S0-AZR-950

The SYBEX Instant Reference Series

Instant References are available on these topics:

AutoCAD Release 12 for DOS

AutoCAD Release 12
for Windows

CorelDRAW 3

dBASE

dBASE IV 1.1 Programmer's

dBASE IV 2.0 Programmer's

DOS 5

DOS 6

DR DOS 6

Excel 4 for Windows

Harvard Graphics 3

Harvard Graphics
for Windows

Lotus 1-2-3 Release 2.3 &
2.4 for DOS

Lotus 1-2-3 for Windows

Microsoft Access

Norton Desktop for DOS

Norton Desktop for
Windows 2.0

Norton Utilities 6

Norton Utilities 7

OS/2 2.1

PageMaker 4.0
for the Macintosh

Paradox 4 Programmer's

Paradox 4 User's

Paradox for Windows User's

PC Tools 8

Quattro Pro for Windows

Windows 3.1

Word for Windows,
Version 2.0

WordPerfect 5.1 for DOS

WordPerfect 5.1 for   Windows

Task	Mouse Action
Resize a graphic	Click the graphic and drag the box in or out.
Cancel a block	Click the left mouse button.
Display pull-down menus	Click the right mouse button.
Navigate menus	Click the menu title and then the command name.
Navigate dialog boxes	Click the option name or the associated graphic element (checkbox, option button, text box). Double-click an item in a list box.
Cancel menus	Click the right mouse button.
Arrange windows	Place the mouse pointer on the title bar of any framed window and drag the window to another location.
Size windows	Place the mouse pointer on the sides, bottom, or corner of any framed window and drag it in or out.

Shortcut Keys

Command	Shortcut
Compose	Ctrl-A
Copy	Ctrl-C
Cut	Ctrl-X
Cycle Through Windows	Ctrl-Y
Exit WP	Home F7
Find Quickmark	Ctrl-F
Go To	Ctrl-Home
Insert Formatted Page Number	Ctrl-P
Italics	Ctrl-I
Macro, Control	Ctrl-PgUp
Normal Font	Ctrl-N
Outline Edit	Ctrl-O
Paste	Ctrl-V
Play Sound Clip	Ctrl-S
Repeat	Ctrl-R
Set Quickmark	Ctrl-Q
Table, Delete Row	Ctrl-Del
Table, Insert Row	Ctrl-Ins
Toggle Text *or* Paragraph Number	Ctrl-T
Undelete	Escape
Undo	Ctrl-Z
WP Characters	Ctrl-W

(Continued on inside back cover)

Computer users are not all alike.
Neither are SYBEX books.

We know our customers have a variety of needs. They've told us so. And because we've listened, we've developed several distinct types of books to meet the needs of each of our customers. What are you looking for in computer help?

If you're looking for the basics, try the **ABC's** series. For a more visual approach, select full-color **Quick & Easy** books.

Running Start books are two books in one: a fast-paced tutorial, followed by a command reference.

Mastering and **Understanding** titles offer you a step-by-step introduction, plus an in-depth examination of intermediate-level features, to use as you progress.

Our **Up & Running** series is designed for computer-literate consumers who want a no-nonsense overview of new programs. Just 20 basic lessons, and you're on your way.

SYBEX **Encyclopedias**, **Desktop References**, and **A to Z** books provide a *comprehensive reference* and explanation of all of the commands, features, and functions of the subject software.

Sometimes a subject requires a special treatment that our standard series don't provide. So you'll find we have titles like **Advanced Techniques, Handbooks, Tips & Tricks,** and others that are specifically tailored to satisfy a unique need.

You'll find SYBEX publishes a variety of books on every popular software package. Looking for computer help? Help Yourself to SYBEX.

For a complete catalog of our publications:

SYBEX Inc.
2021 Challenger Drive, Alameda, CA 94501
Tel: (510) 523-8233/(800) 227-2346 Telex: 336311
Fax: (510) 523-2373

WordPerfect® 6 for DOS®
Instant Reference

Robin Merrin

SYBEX ®

San Francisco • Paris • Düsseldorf • Soest

Acquisitions Editor: Dianne King
Developmental Editor: Steve Lipson
Editor: Peter Weverka
Technical Editor: Sheila Dienes
Project Editor: Michelle Nance
Book Designer: Ingrid Owen
Screen Graphics: Cuong Le
Typesetter/Page Layout: Claudia Smelser
Proofreader/Production Assistant: Kristin M. Amlie
Indexer: Nancy Guenther
Cover Designer: Archer Design
SYBEX is a registered trademark of SYBEX Inc.

Library of Congress Card Number: 93-84820
ISBN: 0-7821-1197-1

Manufactured in the United States of America

10 9 8 7 6 5 4 3 2 1

To Cecile Emily Merrin

Acknowledgments

Several people made significant contributions to this book and I thank them wholeheartedly.

Thomas Merrin did the research and checking to ensure that the manuscript was accurate and the steps would work. He also gets credit for all the screen shots.

Peter Weverka edited the book meticulously. Sheila Dienes performed an exhaustive and tremendously helpful technical edit. Steve Lipson assisted in shaping the book and getting us started. And, Dianne King was kind enough to ask me to write it.

Table of Contents

Introduction *xv*

Introduction

With the release of WordPerfect 6.0, WordPerfect Corporation has added a graphical user interface and many sophisticated features to the most powerful word processing program you can buy.

Who Should Read This Book

Whether you are upgrading to WordPerfect 6.0 from an earlier version or switching from a different word processing program, this book is for you. This alphabetical reference of commands and features will help you find the information you need to complete a task or solve a problem quickly and easily so you can get back to work. And, this book is designed so you can carry it in your briefcase or laptop case, or keep it on your desk and have the answers ready whenever you need them.

If you are new to computers or word processors, you'll probably want to start with one of SYBEX's other books on WordPerfect and turn to this book after you've acquired the basics.

How to Use This Book

This book is an alphabetical reference to WordPerfect's commands and features. In many cases where there isn't a specific command on the menu to carry out a fairly common task, I've included the relevant feature or task as a topic, so you can look it up quickly. If you can't find what you are looking for in the alphabetical listings, the index is sure to have it.

The entries include:

- A brief description of the command or feature
- Step-by-step procedures to complete one or more tasks
- Descriptions of options where relevant
- Tables for easy reference
- Additional notes with useful information to save you time and avoid problems

- Cross references to related entries

- Figures to illustrate how to perform tasks and what many of the new program features are

Step-by-step instructions tell you how to use menus, dialog boxes, shortcut keys, and the mouse. However, keep in mind that if you open a dialog box with the shortcut keys instead of choosing the command from the menu, you'll usually have an extra dialog box to close when you're finished.

For Beginners...

If you are just getting started with WordPerfect 6.0, you'll probably find these entries most helpful:

- Graphics Mode, Page Mode, and Text Mode entries will help you see the differences in the viewing modes and determine which is best for you.

- The Dialog Boxes and Menus entries will help you learn the techniques for selecting commands and options.

- Button Bar, Menu Bar, Outline Bar, Ribbon, Scroll Bars, and Windows will teach you to use multiple windows and window elements.

- Setup will help you to establish your WordPerfect preferences.

WordPerfect 6.0 System Requirements

Before you install WordPerfect 6.0, make sure your computer meets these system requirements:

- An 80268 processor is required; an 80386 or 80486 processor is recommended.

- 480Kb of RAM is required; 520Kb is recommended.

- MS-DOS or PC-DOS Version 3.0 or higher is required; Version 6.0 with the Memory Manager installed is recommended.

- A CGA monitor is required. An EGA, VGA, or SVGA monitor is recommended in order to use the graphical user interface.

- A hard disk with 7Mb to 16Mb of free space is required, depending on the additional macros, graphics, and tutorial files you want to install.

- One high-density floppy disk drive is required to install from disk. It is not required if you install from the network.

- A mouse is recommended but not required.

WordPerfect is network-ready.

Installing WordPerfect 6.0

To install WordPerfect from the DOS prompt (usually C:>), place the disk labeled "Install 1" in the A: or B: drive and follow these steps:

1. Type **a:install** (or **b:install**) and press ↲.

2. Respond to any questions you see on the screen.

3. When you see the installation menu, choose a method for installing the program:

- Choose **S**tandard Installation (1) if you are installing WordPerfect for the first time.

- Choose **C**ustom Installation (2) to install the Word-Perfect files to specific directories.

- Choose **N**etwork Installation (3) if you are a network administrator installing WordPerfect on the network.

- Choose one of the Miscellaneous Options (4–8) to update your hardware or software if you've previously installed WordPerfect 6.0.

4. Follow the instructions and respond to questions you see on the screen.

Starting WordPerfect 6.0

To start WordPerfect from the DOS prompt (usually C:>), follow these steps (if you let WordPerfect modify your AUTOEXEC.BAT file during installation and added the WP60 install directory to your path statement, you can skip step 1):

1. Type **cd wp60** and press ⏎.

2. Type **wp** and press ⏎.

Features New to WordPerfect 6.0

WordPerfect 6.0 includes these new features. Each is described in detail in this book.

New Feature	Description
Bookmark	You can place one or more bookmarks anywhere in a document to make it easier to find those locations later.
Button Bar	The Button Bar gives you quick access to many of the features, commands, and macros you use repeatedly.
Close	You can close the current window with the Close command or by clicking on the Close box.
Dialog Boxes	Whenever additional input or selections are required before a command or operation can be carried out, WordPerfect now displays a dialog box.
Document Information	The Document Information command calculates and displays document information, including the number of characters, words, sentences, and pages in a document.
Fax Services	If you have an internal fax/modem, you can send a WordPerfect document with the Fax Services command.

New Feature	**Description**
File Manager	File Manager provides many commands to help you manage files and navigate through directories.
Grammatik	Grammatik is a WordPerfect utility that provides complete and thorough grammar, spelling, and style checking. Grammatik analyzes your document interactively and helps you correct any errors it finds.
Graphics Mode	Graphics Mode displays the body of your document, both text and graphics, close to how it will look when printed.
Graphics Retrieve	You can retrieve a graphic directly into your document with the Retrieve Image command. WordPerfect converts it if it is not in .WPG format.
Hypertext	Hypertext lets you create a link or "jump" in one document to a bookmark in the same or another document. It also lets you run a macro by selecting marked text within the document.
Image Editor	The Image Editor lets you scale, crop, rotate, and modify the color and fill of many graphic images.
New	The New command lets you start a new document and open it in a new window in one step.
Open	The Open command lets you open an existing document into a new window in one step, without first closing any documents.
Outline Bar	The Outline Bar provides access to many of the commands and options on the Outline menu and in the Outline dialog box.

New Feature	Description
Page Mode	The Page Mode command displays each page of your document, both text and graphics, close to how it will look when printed. Page mode differs from Graphics mode in that headers, footers, footnotes, and endnotes also are displayed.
Print Preview	Print Preview displays each page of your document, both text and graphics, close to how it will look when printed, based on the printer that is currently selected. You cannot edit your document in the Print Preview window, but you can review all the pages of a large document quickly and easily.
QuickFinder	QuickFinder creates special files so that WordPerfect can rapidly search for words and text strings.
QuickList	The QuickList is a list of the files you use most often, organized by type. It can help you open the directory listing associated with the file type, open a specific file, and enter a directory and/or file name in a dialog box.
Repeat	With Repeat, you can have WordPerfect automatically repeat a keystroke, command, or macro. Examples of commands and keys that can be repeated are cursor movement keys, letters, numbers, and symbols.
Ribbon	The Ribbon provides quick access to several WordPerfect display and formatting features.
Screen Setup	Screen Setup lets you change the default setting for many objects WordPerfect displays.

New Feature	Description
Scroll Bars	The horizontal and vertical scroll bars can be used to quickly display another part of the document that is not visible on the screen.
Sound Clip	You can add a sound clip to a document, play it back, and also record a sound clip. You must have a sound card or similar device installed in your computer to use this feature.
Undo	You can reverse many editing actions with Undo. For example, you can restore text to its original location, restore deleted font attributes, delete newly applied attributes, and reset margins and tabs.
Watermarks	You can add multiple watermarks to a document, using either graphics or text.
Zoom	Use Zoom to change the displayed size of text and graphics in the document window.

ADVANCE

Advance lets you position text at a precise location either on the current page or relative to the current cursor location. Advance is especially useful for accurately placing text on a preprinted form or within a graphic.

To Position Text on the Page

1. Move the cursor to the page where you want the advance to begin.

2. From the Layout menu, choose Other (Shift-F8,7).

3. Choose Advance (6).

4. Type the number or letter of the horizontal or vertical position you wish to change.

Left from Cursor (1)	Moves the cursor to the left of its current position by the distance you specify.
Right from Cursor (2)	Moves the cursor to the right of its current position by the distance you specify.
From Left Edge of Page (3)	Places the text at the specified distance from the left of the page, without regard to the current cursor location.
Up from Cursor (4)	Moves the cursor up from its current position by the distance you specify.
Down from Cursor (5)	Moves the cursor down from its current position by the distance you specify.
From Top of Page (6)	Places the text at the specified distance from the top of the page, without regard to the current cursor location.

5. Enter a number to indicate the distance to advance and press ↵. The default unit of measure is inches.

6.   Repeat steps 4 and 5 if you want to specify both a horizontal and vertical position.

7.   Choose OK twice. If you used (Shift-F8,7), you also need to select Close.

8.   Type the text.

You cannot see the cursor move in Text mode. Switch to Graphics Mode (Ctrl-F3,3) or Page Mode (Ctrl-F3,4) to see the results.

● **NOTES**   After you use Advance, all text that follows is placed on the page relative to the new location of the cursor. However, you can use Advance again to specify where you want the remaining text to be placed.

● **SEE ALSO**   Graphics Boxes, Graphics Mode, Page Mode, Units of Measure

APPEND

Append lets you add a selected block of text or a graphic from the current file to the end of another file or to the Clipboard. When you append to the Clipboard, you do not replace the text or graphic already on the Clipboard; you add to the existing contents.

To Add Text or a Graphic to a File

1.   Select (block) the text or graphic to append.

2.   From the Edit menu, choose Append.

3.   Choose To File.

4.   Enter the name of the file to which you want to add the text or graphic.

5.   Choose OK or press ↵.

To combine two files, select all the text in one file and append it to the second file.

To Add Text or a Graphic to the Clipboard

If you are running the WordPerfect Shell 4.0 utility program, you can also append to the Clipboard.

1. Select the text to append.

2. From the Edit menu, choose **A**ppend.

3. Choose To Clipboard.

● **SEE ALSO**   Copy/Copy and Paste, Cut/Cut and Paste/Move, Retrieve, Select

AUTO CODE PLACEMENT

Auto Code Placement causes WordPerfect to place certain formatting codes at the beginning of the paragraph or page, no matter where you insert them in the document. Only formatting codes that typically are applied to a paragraph or page are affected.

To Turn On Auto Code Placement

1. From the File menu, choose Setup (Shift-F1).

2. Choose Environment (3).

3. Select Auto Code Placement (T).

4. Choose OK or press ⏎. If you pressed (Shift-F1,3), you also need to select Close.

● **NOTES**   Examples of formatting codes placed at the beginning of the page are those for Page Numbering, Paper Size, and Header. Formatting codes placed at the beginning of the paragraph include those for Justification, Line Height, and Tab Set. Formatting

codes not affected include those for Bold, the Date and Time function, and Hard Page Break.

● **SEE ALSO**   Codes, Reveal Codes

BACKUP

WordPerfect provides two automatic backup options. Timed backups save files on an ongoing basis and prevent you from losing
your work in the event of a power or computer failure. Original
document backups save the most recent version of a file to disk
whenever you save a newer version.

To Perform Automatic Backups

1.   From the File menu, choose Setup (Shift-F1).

2.   Choose Environment (3).

3.   Select Backup Options (1).

4.   Select either or both of the Backup options.

Timed Document Backup (1)	Makes regular backups on an ongoing basis.
Back Up Original Document (3)	Saves the original document as a backup each time you save and when you exit WordPerfect and save your document.

5.   If you selected Timed Document Backup, also select
        Minutes between Backups (2), enter a number, and press ↵.

6.   Choose OK or press ↵ to close the Backup dialog box.

7.   Choose OK or press ↵ to close the Environment dialog
        box. If you pressed (Shift-F1,3), you also need to select
        Close.

Recovering a Timed Backup

Timed backups are saved in temporary files in the directory where WordPerfect is installed, unless you indicate another directory (see "Notes"). The file opened in the Doc 1 window is saved as WP{WPC}.BK1, the file opened in the Doc 2 window is saved as WP{WPC}.BK2, and so on. When you exit WordPerfect, these temporary files are deleted, but when WordPerfect is interrupted by a computer or power failure, they remain on disk.

When you restart WordPerfect again after such an interruption, you'll see a message that tells you a backup file exists and asks if you want to rename, delete, or open it. It is safest to rename the file *when you see this message* in order to save it. To save the file, choose Rename, enter a file name, and press ↵. Next, open or retrieve the file once the WordPerfect screen is displayed.

Opening an Original Document Backup

Original document backups are always saved in the same directory as the original document and have the same file name, but with a .BK! extension. They remain on-disk until you delete them or overwrite them with a newer backup. You can open or retrieve a file with the .BK! extension as you do any other file. Once you've retrieved it, immediately rename it and change the .BK! extension so you do not accidentally write another backup file over it.

● **NOTES**   You can change the directory where WordPerfect stores timed backups with the Setup option, Location of Files (Shift-F1,5,1).

● **SEE ALSO**   Open, Retrieve, Setup

BINDING OFFSET

Binding Offset adjusts text and margins to accommodate a binding edge, typically at the left or top of a two-sided document.

To Set Up a Binding Edge

1. From the Layout menu, choose Other (Shift-F8,7).

2. Choose Printer Functions (9).

3. Select Binding Offset (2).

4. Press ⏎ to select Binding Offset (Add to Margin) (1). Enter the amount and then press ⏎.

5. Repeat step 3.

6. Select From Edge (2), and then select Left, Right, Top, or Bottom.

7. Choose OK twice. If you used (Shift-F8,7), press ⏎ to choose Close.

You can see the result by switching to Print Preview (Shift-F7,7).

To Delete a Binding Edge

Display the Reveal Codes window and delete the binding edge code or use the following steps.

1. From the Layout menu, choose Other (Shift-F8,7).

2. Choose Printer Functions (9).

3. Select Binding Offset (2).

4. Press ⏎ to select Binding Offset (Add to Margin) (1). Enter 0 as the amount and press ⏎.

5. Press ⏎ twice to select OK. If you used (Shift-F8,7), press ⏎ again to choose Close.

● **NOTES** The binding offset is added or subtracted from the margin settings to achieve the desired effect. The binding edge is increased by the amount you specify. When you select Left, the amount is added to the left margin on odd-numbered pages and to the right margin on even-numbered pages. When Top is selected, the amount is added to the top margin on odd-numbered pages and to the bottom margin on even-numbered pages.

If you are going to bind a one-sided document, simply increase the margin on the intended binding edge instead of using the Binding Offset option.

● **SEE ALSO**   Margins, Print Preview, Units of Measure

BLOCK

You can select a block of text with the keyboard or mouse in order to perform an operation on it. You can also use Block Protect to keep a block of text from being split between two pages.

To Select a Block with the Keyboard

1. Place the cursor at the beginning of the block.

2. From the Edit menu, choose **B**lock (Alt-F4).

3. Press ↓ to move the cursor to the last line of the block and press → as many times as necessary to move to the end of the block. You can also extend the selection block with the Home, End, Page Up, and Page Down keys.

To Select a Block with the Mouse

1. Move the mouse cursor to the beginning of the block.

2. Hold down the left mouse button and drag the mouse cursor to the end of the block. Release the mouse button.

● **NOTES**   The selected block is highlighted and remains highlighted until you press Esc or click the left mouse button to cancel the block. You can apply many WordPerfect commands to a block, including Cut, Copy, Move, Spell Check, and Block Protect.

To Protect a Block

Once a block is selected it can be protected as follows:

1.   From the Layout menu, choose Other (Shift-F8,7).

2.   Select Block Protect (1).

3.   Choose OK or press ↵. Press ↵ twice to select Close if you used (Shift-F8,7).

● **NOTES**   Block Protect is most useful for protecting part of a table or chart. To keep a heading together with the paragraph that follows, use Conditional End of Page.

● **SEE ALSO**   Conditional End of Page, Select, and inside the front cover for Cursor Movement Keys

One or more bookmarks can be placed anywhere in a document so you can easily find those locations later. WordPerfect also lets you place one instant bookmark, called a Quickmark, in a document at a time.

To Place a Quickmark

1.   Move the cursor to the location for the Quickmark.

2.   From the Edit menu, choose Bookmark (Shift-F12).

3.   Choose Set Quickmark (Ctrl-Q).

Ctrl-Q sets the Quickmark at the cursor position in one quick step.

To Find a Quickmark

1.   From the Edit menu, choose Bookmark (Shift-F12).

2.   Choose Find Quickmark (Ctrl-F).

Ctrl-F finds the Quickmark in one quick step.

To Create a Bookmark

You can place multiple bookmarks in a document, but you must give each a unique name so that you can find it later.

1.   Move the cursor to the location for the bookmark or select (block) the text you want for your bookmark.

2.   From the Edit menu, choose Bookmark (Shift-F12).

3.   Choose Create (3).

4.   If the text shown will help you identify the bookmark, choose OK. Otherwise, enter a name for the bookmark and choose OK. (The text shown in the text box is deleted once you begin to type.)

To Find a Bookmark

1.   From the Edit menu, choose Bookmark (Shift F-12).

2.   Highlight the name of the bookmark in the list box.

3.   Choose Find (1).

To Delete a Bookmark

1.   From the Edit menu, choose Bookmark (Shift F-12).

2.   Highlight the name of the bookmark in the list box.

3.   Choose Delete (5).

4.   Choose Yes or press Tab and then ⏎ to remove the bookmark.

5.   Choose OK or press Tab and then ↵ to close the dialog box.

● **NOTES**   The Bookmark dialog box also contains options for moving, renaming, and searching for a bookmark.

BORDERS

Borders lets you place a border around selected text, a paragraph, column, table, or page.

To Create a Border

1.   Position the cursor within the paragraph, column, or page where you want to place a border, or select a block of text.

2.   From the Graphics menu, choose Borders (Alt-F9,3).

3.   Choose where you want to place the border.

Paragraph (1)   The current paragraph and all subsequent paragraphs will have the selected border.

Page (2)   The current page and all subsequent pages will have the selected border.

Column (3)   The current column—and optionally the entire table—will have the selected border.

4.   Select Border Style (1).

5.   Highlight a border style in the list box and choose Select (1).

6.   Select Fill Style (2).

7.   Highlight a fill style in the list box and choose Select (1).

8.   Choose OK or press ↵.

● **NOTES**   To place a border around an entire table, select Column Border (Outside and Between) from the Border Style list box. To place a border between columns only, select Column Border (Between only) from the Border Styles list box.

To Turn Off a Border

1.   Position the cursor where you want to turn off the border.

2.   From the **G**raphics menu, choose **B**orders (Alt-F9,3).

3.   Choose the type of border you want to turn off.

4.   Select **O**ff.

● **SEE ALSO**   Columns, Graphics Boxes, Tables

N E W

BUTTON BAR

The WordPerfect Button Bar can give you quick access to many of the features, commands and macros you use repeatedly. However, you can use the Button Bar only if you have a mouse.

To Display the Default Button Bar

1.   From the **V**iew menu, choose **B**utton Bar.

2.   To change the way the button bar is displayed, choose Button Bar **S**etup from the **V**iew menu and choose **O**ptions.

3.   Change the position to **L**eft or **R**ight to display a greater number of buttons.

4.   Also, change the Style to **P**icture and Text (5), Picture **O**nly (6), or **T**ext Only (7). The Text Only option displays the most buttons.

5. Press ↵ to choose OK.

Figure 1 illustrates the standard WordPerfect 6.0 Button Bar displayed vertically in Text and Picture, Picture Only, and Text Only Style.

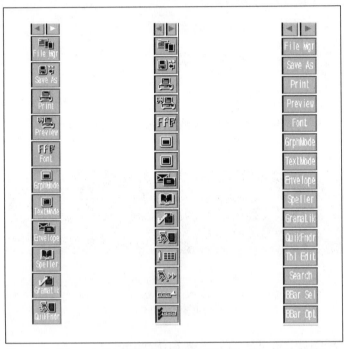

Figure 1: The standard WordPerfect 6.0 Button Bar displayed in Graphics mode in—from left to right—Text and Picture, Picture Only, and Text Only style.

To Select another Button Bar

1. From the View menu, choose Button Bar Setup.

2. Choose Select.

3. Highlight a button bar in the list box and choose Select (1).

To Modify the Current Button Bar

1. From the View menu, choose Button Bar Setup.

2. Choose Edit.

3. Select Add Menu Item (1) to add an item from the menu. The menus become available so you can then select (click) the menu item.

4. Select Add Feature (2) to add a feature not displayed on the menus. WordPerfect opens a list box so you can select from additional features.

5. Select Add Macro (3) to add a macro, and select the macro from the list.

New buttons are added to the end of the Button Bar. Use Move Button (6) to move them to a new location.

6. In the list box, highlight a button that you want to remove and select Move Button (6). Highlight the new location for the button and select Paste Button (6).

7. In the list box, highlight a button that you want to remove, choose Delete (5), and then select Yes to delete the button.

8. When you are finished modifying the Button Bar, choose OK or press Tab, and then press ↵.

To Create a New Button Bar

1. From the View menu, choose Button Bar Setup.

2. Choose Select.

3. Select Create (2).

4. Type a name for the new Button Bar and press ↵.

5. Follow steps 3 through 4 under "To Modify the Current Button Bar" to add buttons to the new Button Bar, or select OK.

● **NOTES**   WordPerfect provides standard Button Bars for the document window and also for the Print Preview window, the

Image Editor, and the Equation Editor. Choose Button Bar from the View menu to display the associated Button Bar when you switch to any of these modes if the associated Button Bar is not currently displayed.

● **SEE ALSO** Equations, Image Editor, Macros, Print Preview

CANCEL

WordPerfect lets you cancel most operations, restore deleted text, and close menus and dialog boxes with its Cancel key and Cancel button.

To Cancel Menus, Dialog Boxes, and Operations

- Press Esc, or
- Click the Cancel button in dialog boxes.

● **NOTES** You may have to press Esc or click Cancel more than once to back out of cascading menus or multiple dialog boxes and return to the document window.

● **SEE ALSO** Dialog Boxes, Menus, Undelete, Undo

CENTER PAGE

Center Page lets you center all text on the page between the top and bottom margin. You can center text on the current page or all pages.

To Center Text Vertically on the Page

1. Position the cursor on the page you want to center.

2. From the Layout menu, choose Page (Shift-F8,3).

3. Choose either Center Current Page (2) or Center Pages (3).

4. Choose OK or press ↵ to close the dialog box. If you used (Shift-F8,3), you also need to select Close.

● **NOTES**   To turn off Center Page, follow the same steps, but select Center Current Page or Center Pages to remove the check.

If Auto Code Placement is not turned on, you'll need to place the cursor at the top of the page to be centered. Headers and Footers are not affected by Center Page.

● **SEE ALSO**   Auto Code Placement, Center Text, Headers and Footers, Justification

CENTER TEXT

You can center a single line or a block of text between the left and right margins by using the Center command on the Alignment menu.

To Center a Line

You can center text before or after you type it in. To center it before you type:

1. Place the cursor at the beginning of the line where you will type the text.

2. From the Layout menu, choose Alignment, and then choose Center (Shift-F6).

3. Type the text and press ↵ to complete the centering.

If the text is already entered:

1.   Place the cursor at the beginning of the line.

2.   From the Layout menu, choose **A**lignment, and then choose **C**enter (Shift-F6).

To Center a Block

1.   Select the block of text you want to center.

2.   From the Layout menu, choose **J**ustification.

3.   Choose **C**enter.

To Center Text in Columns

1.   Place the cursor at the left margin of the column.

2.   From the Layout menu, choose **A**lignment, and then choose **C**enter (Shift-F6).

3.   Type the text and press ↵ to complete the centering.

● **NOTES**   To center text at a specific location that is not the center of the page, place the cursor at that point before choosing Center.

● **SEE ALSO**   Center Page, Justification, Select

CODES

WordPerfect inserts hidden codes into your document when you use most formatting features. These codes determine how your document will look when printed.

● **NOTES**   Codes that affect a block of text are inserted as a pair of on/off codes. For example,

[Italc On]**Super Value Sale!**[Italc Off]

causes the words *Super Value Sale!* to print in italics; other text remains unaffected. Some codes are inserted individually, not in pairs. For example, [HRt] shows that a Hard Return has been placed at the end of the line.

You can delete most formatting within a document by deleting the hidden code. Table 1 shows WordPerfect 6.0 formatting codes. You can view these codes in your document with the Reveal Codes command.

● **SEE ALSO**   Delete, Reveal Codes

Table 1: WordPerfect 6.0 Formatting Codes

Code	Definition
-	Hard Hyphen (Character)
[- Hyphen]	Hyphen
[- Soft Hyphen]	Soft Hyphen
[- Soft Hyphen EOL]	Soft Hyphen at End of Line
[Auto Hyphen EOL]	Automatic Hyphen at End of Line
[Back Tab]	Back Tab (Margin Release)
[Bar Code]	Bar Code
[Begin Gen Txt]	Beginning of Generated Text
[Binding Width]	Binding Width
[Block]	Block
[Block Pro]*	Block Protection
[Bold]*	Bold
[Bookmark]	Bookmark
[Bot Mar]	Bottom Margin
[Box Num]	Box Number
[Calc Col]	Calculation Column
[Cancel Hyph]	Cancel Word Hyphenation
[Cell]	Table Cell

18   Codes

Table 1: WordPerfect 6.0 Formatting Codes (continued)

Code	Definition
[Change BOL/EOL Char]	Change Beginning or End of Line Character
[Chap Num]	Chapter Number
[Char Box]	Character Box
[Char Shade Change]	Character Shade Change
[Char Style]*	Character Style
[Cntr Cur Pg]	Center Current Page Vertically
[Cntr on Cur Pos]	Center on Cursor Position
[Cntr on Mar]	Center on Margins
[Cntr Pgs]	Center Pages Vertically
[CNTR TAB]	Hard Centered Tab
[Cntr Tab]	Centered Tab
[Col Border]	Column Border
[Col Def]	Column Definition
[Color]	Print Color
[Comment]	Document Comment
[Condl EOP]	Conditional End of Page
[Count]	Counter
[Date]	Date and Time Function
[Date Fmt]	Date and Time Format
[Dbl Und]*	Double Underline
[Dbl-Sided Print]	Double-Sided Printing
[DEC TAB]	Hard Decimal-Aligned Tab
[Dec Tab]	Decimal-Aligned Tab
[Dec/Align Char]	Decimal/Alignment Character
[Def Mark]	Definition Marker
[Delay]*	Delay
[Do Grand Tot]	Calculate Grand Total

Table 1: WordPerfect 6.0 Formatting Codes (continued)

Code	Definition
[Do Subtot]	Calculate Subtotal
[Do Total]	Calculate Total
[Dorm HRt]	Dormant Hard Return
[Dot Lead Char]	Dot Leader Character
[End Cntr/Align]	End of Centering/Alignment
[End Gen Txt]	End of Generated Text
[Endnote]	Endnote
[Endnote Min]	Endnote Minimum Amount
[Endnote Num]	Endnote Number
[Endnote Placement]	Endnote Placement
[Endnote Space]	Endnote Spacing
[Ext Large]*	Extra Large Font Size
[Filename]	File Name
[Fine]*	Fine Font Size
[First Ln Ind]	First Line Indent
[Flsh Rgt]	Flush Right
[Flt Cell Begin]	Floating Cell Begin
[Flt Cell End]	Floating Cell End
[Font]	Font
[Font Size]	Font Size
[Footer A/B]	Footer A or B
[Footer Sep]	Footer Separator Space
[Footnote]	Footnote
[Footnote Cont Msg]	Footnote Continued Message
[Footnote Min]	Footnote Minimum Amount
[Footnote Num]	Footnote Number
[Footnote Sep Ln]	Footnote Separator Line
[Footnote Space]	Footnote Spacing

Table 1: WordPerfect 6.0 Formatting Codes (continued)

Code	Definition
[Footnote Txt Pos]	Footnote Text Position
[Force]	Force Odd/Even Page
[Formatted Pg Num]	Formatted Page Number
[Graph Line]	Graphics Line
[HAdv]	Horizontal Advance
[HCol]	Hard Column Break
[Header A/B]	Header A or B
[Header Sep]	Header Separator Space
[Hidden]*	Hidden Text
[Hidden Txt]	Hidden Body Text in an Outline
[HPg]	Hard Page Break
[HRow]	Hard Table Row
[HRt]	Hard Return
[HSpace]	Hard Space
[Hypertext Begin]	Hypertext Begin
[Hypertext End]	Hypertext End
[Hyph]	Hyphenation
[Index]	Index Entry
[Italc]*	Italics
[Just]	Justification
[Just Lim]	Word Spacing Justification Limits
[Kern]	Kerning
[Labels Form]	Labels Form
[Lang]	Language
[Large]*	Large Font Size
[Leading Adj]	Leading Adjustment
[Lft HZone]	Left Edge of Hyphenation Zone
[Lft Indent]	Left Indent

Table 1: WordPerfect 6.0 Formatting Codes (continued)

Code	Definition
[Lft Mar]	Left Margin
[Lft Mar Adj]	Left Margin Adjustment
[LFT TAB]	Hard Left-Aligned Tab
[Lft Tab]	Left-Aligned Tab
[Lft/Rgt Indent]	Double Indent
[Link]	Spreadsheet Link
[Link End]	Spreadsheet Link End
[Ln Height]	Line Height
[Ln Num]	Line Numbering
[Ln Spacing]	Line Spacing
[Macro Func]	Macro Function
[Math]	Math On
[Math Def]	Definition of Math Columns
[Math Neg]	Math Negate
[MRG:*command*]	Merge Programming Command
[Mrk Txt List Begin]	Beginning of List Entry
[Mrk Txt List End]	End of List Entry
[Mrk Txt ToC Begin]	Beginning of Table of Contents Entry
[Mrk Txt ToC End]	End of Table of Contents Entry
[Open Style]	Open Style
[Outline]	Outline
[Outln]*	Outline Attribute
[Ovrstk]*	Overstrike
[Paper Sz/Typ]	Paper Size and Type
[Para Border]	Paragraph Border
[Para Box]	Paragraph Box
[Para Num]	Paragraph Number
[Para Spacing]	Paragraph Spacing

Table 1: WordPerfect 6.0 Formatting Codes (continued)

Code	Definition
[Para Style]	Paragraph Style
[Para Style End]	Paragraph Style End
[Pause Ptr]	Pause Printer
[Pg Border]	Page Border
[Pg Box]	Page Box
[Pg Num]	Page Number
[Ptr Cmnd]	Printer Command
[Redln]*	Redline
[Ref]	Cross-Reference
[Rgt HZone]	Right Edge of Hyphenation Zone
[Rgt Mar]	Right Margin
[Rgt Mar Adj]	Right Margin Adjustment
[RGT TAB]	Hard Right-Aligned Tab
[Rgt Tab]	Right-Aligned Tab
[Row]	Table Row
[Sec Pg Num]	Secondary Page Number
[Shadw]*	Shadow
[Sm Cap]*	Small Caps
[Small]*	Small Font Size
[Sound]	Sound Clip
[Speller/Grammatik]	Spell/Grammatik in Use
[SPg]	Soft Page Break
[SRt]	Soft Return
[StkOut]*	Strikeout
[Subdivided Pg]	Subdivided Page
[Subdoc]	Subdocument in Master Document
[Subdoc Begin	Beginning of Subdocument
[Subdoc End]	End of Subdocument

Table 1: WordPerfect 6.0 Formatting Codes (continued)

Code	Definition
[Subscpt]*	Subscript
[Subtot Entry]	Subtotal Entry
[Suppress]	Suppress Header, Footer, Watermark, or Page Number
[Suprscpt]*	Superscript
[Tab Set]	Tab Set
[Target]	Cross-Reference Target
[Tbl Dec Tab]	Table Decimal Tab
[Tbl Def]	Table Definition
[Tbl Off]	Table Off
[Tbl Tab]	Table Tab
[THCol]	Temporary Hard Column Break
[Third Party]	Non-WordPerfect Code
[Thousands Char]	Thousands Character
[THPg]	Temporary Hard Page Break
[THRt]	Temporary Hard Return
[ToA]	Table of Authorities Entry
[Top Mar]	Top Margin
[Total Entry]	Total Entry
[TSRt]	Temporary Soft Return
[Und]*	Underline
[Undrln Space]	Underline Spaces
[Undrln Tab]	Underline Tabs
[Unknown]	Unknown Code
[VAdv]	Vertical Advance
[Very Large]*	Very Large Font Size
[Vol Num]	Volume Number
[Watermark A/B]	Watermark A or B

Table 1: WordPerfect 6.0 Formatting Codes (continued)

Code	Definition
[Wid/Orph]	Widow/Orphan Protect
[Wrd/Ltr Spacing]	Word and Letter Spacing

* Inserted as a pair of on/off codes. This code will be followed by the word on or off.

COLUMNS

Use the Columns command to format text into one or more columns on the page.

To Define Columns

You can set up columns before or after you enter text. If the text has already been entered, place the cursor in front of it before defining the columns.

1.   From the Layout menu, choose Columns (Alt-F7,1).

2.   Select Column Type (1), and select a column type:

Newspaper (1)   Text flows to the bottom of the page in each column and from the bottom of one column to the top of the next.

Balanced Newspaper (2)   Text flows from the bottom of one column to the top of the next, but the columns on each page are of equal height.

Parallel (3)	Blocks of text are held together side-by-side and a single column can be longer than one page.
Parallel with **B**lock Protect (4)	Each set of columns is held together side-by-side on a page.

3. Select **N**umber of Columns (2), type a number in the text box, and press ↵.

4. To change the amount of space between columns, select **D**istance Between Columns (3), type a number, and press ↵.

5. To change the amount of space between rows, select Line **S**pacing Between Rows (4), type a number, and press ↵.

6. If you want to add a border, select Column **B**orders (5), make those selections in the dialog box, and choose OK.

7. Choose OK or press ↵.

To Turn Columns On

You can quickly turn columns on when the Ribbon is displayed.

1. Place the cursor at the beginning of the text.

2. Point to the Column button with the mouse. Press and hold the left mouse button, drag the mouse to select the number of columns, and release the mouse button.

When you turn columns on with the Ribbon, WordPerfect creates evenly spaced newspaper-style columns.

To Turn Columns Off

1. Place the cursor within the columns.

2. From the Layout menu, choose **C**olumns (Alt-F7,1).

3. Choose Off. If you used (Alt-F-7, 1), you also need to select OK.

To Move between Columns

To move between columns with the keyboard in order to edit, press Ctrl-Home and either ← or →. If you are using a mouse, click anywhere in any column in order to move the cursor.

● **NOTES**   When creating newspaper-style columns, you can begin a new column by inserting a Hard Page break. From the Layout menu, choose Alignment, and then choose Hard Page (Ctrl-↵).

If you insert a Hard Page break in parallel columns, all text and codes after the break move to the next column. Use Reveal Codes to make sure you place the break correctly.

If additional lines appear at the top of columns, delete any extra Hard Returns.

● **SEE ALSO**   Borders, Reveal Codes, Ribbon, Tables, and inside the front cover for Cursor Movement Keys

COMMENTS

You can insert hidden text in a document by creating a comment. The text appears on the screen but is not printed.

To Add a Comment to a Document

1.   Place the cursor where you want to enter the comment.

2.   From the Layout menu, choose Comment (Ctrl-F7,2).

3.   Choose Create (1).

4.   Type the text and press F7 when you're done.

To Edit a Comment

1. Place the cursor right after the comment.

2. From the Layout menu, choose Comment (Ctrl-F7,2).

3. Choose Edit (2).

4. Edit the text and press F7.

To Convert a Comment to Text

Later, you can convert an existing comment to text in order to print it as part of your document.

1. Place the cursor right after the comment.

2. From the Layout menu, choose Comment (Ctrl-F7,2).

3. Choose Convert to Text (3).

To Convert Text to a Comment

You can also convert text already entered in your document to a comment in order to prevent it from being printed.

1. Select (block) the text you want to convert.

2. From the Layout menu, choose Comment (Ctrl-F7,2).

3. Choose Create (1).

● **NOTES**   Comments are especially helpful for collecting notes or feedback on a document and for saving information related to a document.

● **SEE ALSO**   Select

COMPARE DOCUMENTS

Compare Documents lets you compare two versions of a document and have WordPerfect mark the differences. You can compare an on-screen document to a version on disk; the differences are marked in the on-screen version.

To Compare Two Documents

Before you begin the Compare, open the first document in the document window.

1. From the File menu, choose Compare Documents, and then choose Add Markings (Alt-F5,8).

2. Choose Document on Disk (1) to display a text box.

3. Enter the name of the file that is to be compared to the open file and press ⏎.

4. Select a Compare by method (2) and press ⏎.

WordPerfect compares individual segments of the document based on the option you select from the following list of commands:

Word (1)	Words are separated by single spaces.
Phrase (2)	Phrases are separated by punctuation such as commas, colons, and semicolons, in addition to the sentence markers.
Sentence (3)	Sentence markers include periods, question marks, and Hard Returns.
Paragraph (4)	Paragraphs are separated by a Hard Return.

5. Choose OK or press ⏎.

A dialog box shows the progress of the compare operation. When completed, the document window displays the results.

To Delete Document Markings

Once you have seen the results of a document compare, you can delete the markings, if you wish.

1. From the File menu, choose Compare Documents, and then choose Remove Markings (Alt-F5,9).

2. At the prompt, select OK or press ↵.

● **NOTES**   Changes are marked in the on-screen document. Changes include those found in footnotes, endnotes, and tables. Changes in headers, footers, and graphic boxes are not marked, as they are not included in the compare operation.

● **SEE ALSO**   Open, Redlining and Strikeout, Retrieve

CONDITIONAL END OF PAGE

Conditional End of Page lets you keep a specific number of lines together on a page.

To Specify Lines to Be Kept Together

Use Conditional End of Page to prevent an awkward page break, especially between headings and the text that follows.

1. Place the cursor on the line that precedes the lines you want to keep together.

2. From the Layout menu, choose Other (Shift-F8,7).

3. Choose Conditional End of Page (2).

4. In the Number of Lines to Keep Together text box, type the number and press ↵.

5. Choose OK or press ↵. If you used (Shift-F-8,7), you also need to select Close.

● **NOTES** Remember to account for blank lines, especially in double- or triple-spaced documents, when you count the number of lines to protect.

When you want to protect a block of text from an unwanted page break, use block protect instead.

● **SEE ALSO** Block

CONVERT CASE

Convert Case lets you convert selected text to uppercase, lowercase, or initial caps. With initial caps, the first letter in each word is capitalized.

To Convert Text

1. Select the block of text you want to convert.
2. From the Edit menu, choose Convert Case (Shift-F3).
3. Choose one of the three options: Uppercase (1), Lowercase (2), or Initial caps (3).

● **NOTES** WordPerfect recognizes the first word of each sentence and capitalizes it when you convert to lowercase. By including punctuation from the preceding sentence in your block, you can make sure that the first word in a sentence is properly capitalized as well. The word I and its contractions (I'm, I'll) are also properly capitalized.

If you press Shift-F3 when no text is selected, the Switch command is activated.

● **SEE ALSO** Block, Select

CONVERT FILE

You can convert files created in other applications so you can edit them in WordPerfect. You can also convert files to many formats recognized by other word processing applications.

To Import a File from another Format

1. From the File menu, choose **O**pen or **R**etrieve (Shift-F10).

2. Enter the name—and the path too, if necessary—of the file to import. If the file is not in WordPerfect format, a list of formats you can convert from is displayed.

3. If it is not highlighted already, highlight the current file format in the list box.

4. Choose Select or press ↵.

Once the file is converted it is opened in the document window.

To Export a File to another Format

1. From the File menu, choose Save **A**s (F10).

2. Type a different file name if necessary.

3. Select an application from the Format drop-down list box (2).

4. Choose OK or press ↵.

● **NOTES** Files created in WordPerfect 5.1 for DOS or Windows are automatically converted when you open them in WordPerfect 6.0.

● **SEE ALSO** Open, Retrieve, Save/Save As

COPY/COPY AND PASTE

Copy places a copy of the selected text or graphic in a WordPerfect buffer so you can later paste it within the current or another document. Copy and Paste immediately copies the selected text or graphic to another location.

To Copy Text or a Graphic

1. Select the text or graphic to copy.

2. From the Edit menu, choose Copy (Ctrl-C).

When you copy to a buffer, you replace the previous contents.

To Paste Text or a Graphic

1. Place the cursor where you want to insert the text or graphic.

2. From the Edit menu, choose Paste (Ctrl-V).

You can copy the text or graphic in the buffer to one or more documents an unlimited number of times.

To Copy and Paste

1. Select the text or graphic to copy.

2. From the Edit menu, choose Copy and Paste (Ctrl-Ins).

3. Place the cursor where you want to insert the text or graphic and press ↵. If you want to paste to another document, use the Open command to open the document. If the document is already open in another window, use the Switch To command to display it.

You can also copy text or a graphic by selecting it and then pressing Ctrl while you drag it to its new location with the mouse.

• **NOTES**   Once you use Copy and Paste, you can use Paste again to insert the text or graphic at additional locations; the text or graphic remains in the buffer until it is replaced or you exit WordPerfect.

• **SEE ALSO**   Cut/Cut and Paste/Move, Open, Select, Windows

CROSS-REFERENCE

Cross-Reference is used to automatically update page references to information, figures, illustrations, and notes on other pages. A reference refers the reader to another place in the document. For example, *see Page 5* and *refer to Figure 2–3* are references.

To Mark the Reference

1. Place the cursor where you want to insert the reference.

2. Type the text to precede the reference. For example, you could type *see page* and add a space.

3. From the Tools menu, choose Cross-Reference (Alt-F5,1).

4. Select Reference or Cross-Reference (4).

5. Select a type from the Tie Reference to (1) list. Nine types of items can be cross-referenced: Page, Secondary Page, Chapter, Volume, Paragraph/Outline, Footnote, Endnote, Caption Number, and Counter.

6. Type a name in the Target Name (2) text box and press ↵.

7. Press ↵ again to select OK. A question mark will appear in the location of the marked reference.

You must mark the Reference separately when it is located in a graphics box caption, header, or footer.

To Mark the Target

The target is the place in the document that you want the reader to turn to. You give the target a name in order to identify it.

1. Place the cursor to the immediate right of the target.

2. From the **Tools** menu, choose Cross-Reference and then choose **Target** (Alt-F5,1,5).

3. Type the name of the target and choose OK, or press ↵.

To Mark both the Reference and Target

1. Place the cursor where you want to insert the reference.

2. Type the text to precede the reference. For example, you could type *see page* and add a space.

3. From the **Tools** menu, choose Cross-Reference and then choose **Both** (Alt-F5,1,6).

4. Select a type from the Tie **Reference** to (1) list.

5. Type a name in the **Target** Name (2) text box and press ↵.

6. Choose OK.

7. Place the cursor to the immediate right of the target and press ↵. The page number of the reference appears.

To Generate the Cross-Reference

After you've placed all the references and targets, you can generate the cross-reference.

1. From the **Tools** menu, choose Generate (Alt-F5,4).

2. Choose OK or press ↵.

Remember to use Generate again after editing your document and before printing it.

Inserting Multiple References

You can cross-reference the same target with more than one reference by inserting multiple references at different locations. You can also cross-reference the same target with more than one reference type, as in the example *see page 20, table 5*. You'll need to insert the references for each different type.

You can also place references at a single location to several targets, as in the example *see Figure 8 and Figure 9*. You'll only need to mark the reference once, but you'll need to create multiple targets separately, each with the same target name.

Marking Targets

When you mark a target that is not text—for example, a graphics box or a paragraph number—place the cursor to the immediate right of the code before inserting the target. When marking a page reference, place the target within the text; it does not have to be to the right.

When marking a page number for a footnote or endnote, the corresponding editing window must be active. Before you mark a page number for an endnote, first generate the endnotes so that the referenced page numbers are correct.

● **SEE ALSO** Footnotes and Endnotes, Graphics Boxes, Outline, Page Numbering, Paragraph Numbering, Reveal Codes

CUT/CUT AND PASTE/MOVE

Cut deletes the selected text or graphic and places it in the Word-Perfect buffer so you can later paste it within the current or another document. Copy and Paste immediately moves the selected text or graphic to another location.

To Cut (Delete) Text or a Graphic

1.   Select the text or graphic to cut.

2.   From the Edit menu, choose Cut (Ctrl-X).

When you cut, you replace the previous buffer contents.

To Paste Text or a Graphic

1.   Place the cursor where you want to insert the text or graphic.

2.   From the Edit menu, choose Paste (Ctrl-V).

You can copy the text or graphic in the buffer to one or more documents an unlimited number of times.

To Move (Cut and Paste)

1.   Select the text or graphic to move.

2.   From the Edit menu, choose Cut and Paste (Ctrl-Del).

3.   Place the cursor where you want to move the text or graphic. If you want to move to another document, use the File Open command to open the document. If the document is already open in another window, use the Window Switch To command to display it.

4.   Press ↵.

You can also move text or a graphic by selecting it and then dragging it to its new location with the mouse.

● **NOTES**   Once you use Cut and Paste, you can use Paste again to insert the text or graphic at additional locations. Text or a graphic remains in the buffer until it is replaced or you exit WordPerfect.

● **SEE ALSO**   Copy/Copy and Paste, Delete, Open, Select, Windows

DATE AND TIME

With the Date command, you can insert the current date and time or insert a code that updates the date and time whenever you open or print your document.

To Insert the Date and Time

1. Place the cursor where you want to insert the date.

2. From the Tools menu, choose Date (Shift-F5).

3. Choose (Insert Date) Text (1) to insert the current date, or choose (Insert Date) Code (2) to insert a code that automatically adjusts the date each time you open or print the document.

Today's date is inserted at the cursor location. If you selected Text, this date will not change the next time you open or print the document.

To Change the Date and Time Format

You can quickly change the date and time format for the current document.

1. From the Tools menu, choose Date (Shift-F5).

2. Choose (Date) Format (3).

3. Select any of the predefined formats and choose OK.
   If you want to create a custom format:

   1. Choose Edit (9).

   2. Press Delete several times to delete the code from the Edit text box.

   3. Select, in the order you want them to appear, one or more codes from the Date Codes (F-5) and Time Codes (Shift-F5) list boxes.

4. In the Edit (1) text box, enter any punctuation and spaces you want included. The Date Preview text box shows how the date will look, based on the codes and punctuation you enter. WordPerfect cursor movement and editing keys are available for editing the codes in the Edit text box.

4. When you are satisfied with the format change, press ↵.

5. Choose OK.

● **NOTES**   You also can change the default date and time format for all documents by using Initial Codes.

● **SEE ALSO**   Delete, Initial Codes, and inside the front cover for Cursor Movement Keys

DECIMAL ALIGNMENT

The Character Format command lets you change the decimal alignment character used in tables and tabs and the thousands-separator character used in math calculations.

To Change the Decimal Alignment or Thousands Separator-Character

1. From the Layout menu, choose Character (Shift-F8,6).

2. To change the decimal alignment character, select Decimal/Align Character (1) and type a replacement character in the text box.

3. To change the thousands-separator character, select Thousands Separator (2) and type a replacement character in the text box.

4. Choose OK or press ⏎. If you used (Shift-F8, 6), you also need to select Close.

● **NOTES** You also can change the decimal alignment and thousands-separator characters for all documents by using Initial Codes.

● **SEE ALSO** Initial Codes, Math, Tables, Tabs

DELETE

You can delete text, graphics, or codes with the Cut command or by using any of WordPerfect's keystroke combinations for deleting.

To Delete Text or Graphics

1. Select the block of text or graphic you want to delete.

2. Press Delete or Backspace.

To Delete Codes

1. From the View menu, choose Reveal Codes (Alt-F3).

2. Place the cursor to the left of the code you want to delete and press Delete, or place the cursor to the right of the code you want to delete and press Backspace. When deleting a pair of codes, you only have to delete one; Word-Perfect deletes the other automatically.

Table 2 shows WordPerfect key combinations that let you delete blocks of text.

● **NOTES** You can restore deleted text, graphics, and codes with Undelete and Undo. You also can delete codes or text by searching for them.

Table 2: WordPerfect Delete Keys

Key(s)	Deletes
Backspace	One character to the left of the cursor.
Delete	One character to the right of the cursor in Page mode or Graphics mode. Deletes the character at the cursor in Text mode.
Ctrl-Delete	The entire word in which the cursor lies and any codes within the word.
Ctrl-Backspace	The entire word in which the cursor lies and any codes within the text.
Home-Backspace	All characters and codes from the cursor to the beginning of the word.
Home-Delete	All characters and codes from the cursor to the end of the word.
Ctrl-End	All characters and codes from the cursor to the end of the line.
Ctrl-Page Down	All characters and codes from the cursor to the end of the page.

● **SEE ALSO**   Block, Cut/Cut and Paste/Move, Reveal Codes, Search, Select, Undelete, Undo

N E W

DIALOG BOXES

Whenever additional input or selections are required before a command or operation can be carried out, WordPerfect displays a dialog box.

The Font dialog box shown in Figures 2 and 3 presents many different options and immediately shows you the result of your selections.

To Move Around and Select Options with the Keyboard

- Press the highlighted or underlined letter within the option.
- Press the number or letter that precedes the option.

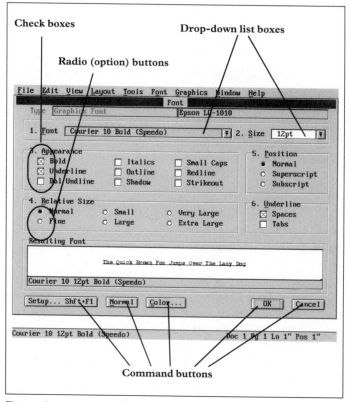

Figure 2: The Font dialog box in Graphics and Page mode

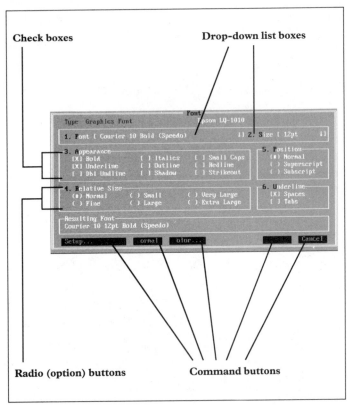

Figure 3: The Font dialog box in Text mode

- Press Tab to move forward or Shift-Tab to move backward through the available options. Then press ↵ to activate an option group and use the arrow keys to move through an option group. Press the spacebar to toggle an option on or off.

- To select the default item in a dialog box, press ↵. In Graphics mode and Page mode, the default item is always displayed with a dotted outline. In Text mode, the default item is highlighted or in a contrasting color.

If an option you want to select does not currently have a number or highlighted letter displayed, press Tab.

To Move Around and Select with the Mouse

- Click the option name or the associated graphic element (the check box, option button, or text box).

To Close a Dialog Box

To close a dialog and have your selections take effect, choose the OK button:

- With the keyboard, press Tab until OK is the default (surrounded by a dotted outline or highlighted), and then press ↵.

- Click OK at any time.

To close a dialog box and cancel all your selections:

- Press Esc. (You may have to press Esc twice.)

- With the keyboard, press Tab until Cancel or Close is the default (surrounded by a dotted outline or highlighted), and then press ↵.

- Click Cancel or Close at any time.

- Press Home and then F7 to close all open dialog boxes at one time.

● **NOTES**   When you select a text box option, you can type directly into the text box. WordPerfect cursor movement and editing keys are available for editing. When an option is unavailable, it is dimmed. When an option opens another dialog box, an ellipsis (…) is shown.

Table 3 summarizes the components of a dialog box. A dialog box can contain any combination of these items.

● **SEE ALSO**   Cancel, and inside the front cover for Cursor Movement Keys

Table 3: Dialog Box Components

Item	Purpose
Text box	Lets you enter text. For example, you could enter the name of a file to open, or retrieve, or a number.
Spin buttons	When spin buttons are displayed to the right of a text box, you can press ↑ or ↓ to scroll numbers in the text box instead of typing a number.
List box	Displays all the possible selections. A scroll bar is also displayed if all items in the list do not fit on the screen. Use the scroll bar or the ↓ or ↑ to scroll the list.
Drop-down list box	Displays available selections when you click the prompt button to the right of the text box.
Pop-up list box	Displays available selections when you press and hold the mouse button over it.
Check box	A box with an X in it means an option is selected; an empty check box means it is not selected. More than one option may be checked within a dialog box.
Radio (option) button	In Graphics mode or Page mode, a black center means an option is selected; a white center means it is not selected. In Text mode, an unselected radio button is empty. Only one radio button may be selected within a group but more than one radio button may be selected within a dialog box. Radio buttons are also called option buttons.
Command button	Displays a command to be carried out. OK and Cancel are the most common command buttons.

DISPLAY PITCH

Display Pitch lets you manually adjust how text is displayed on-screen so that text does not overlap or run off the right side of the screen.

To Change the Display Pitch

The display pitch can be changed anywhere in the document. Once it is changed, the entire document is affected.

1. From the Layout menu, choose Document (Shift-F8,4).

2. Choose Display Pitch (7).

3. Enter a number in the Display Pitch text box. If the columns are too far apart, enter a higher number than the one shown. If the columns overlap, enter a lower number. Then press ↵.

4. Select Manual (2).

5. Choose OK or press ↵.

The change can only be seen in Text mode. If the change is too great or small, repeat the steps until you find exactly the right number to achieve the desired results.

● **NOTES**   The number in the Display Pitch text box shows how much space is allotted to formatting elements such as indents, tabs, and table or column margins that use absolute measurements. It does not affect the space between characters. A display pitch of 0.1 will cause a one-inch indent to be 10 characters wide on-screen. A display pitch of 0.25 will cause the same indent to be 4 characters wide.

● **SEE ALSO**   Columns, Text Mode

DOCUMENT INFORMATION

WordPerfect can automatically calculate some handy document statistics whenever you need them. The Document Information command calculates and displays countable document information, including the number of characters, words, sentences, and pages.

To View Document Information

1. From the Tools menu, choose Writing Tools (Alt-F1).

2. Choose Document Info (4). WordPerfect calculates and then displays the information in a dialog box.

3. To close the dialog box, choose OK or press ↵.

To view the document information in one step, press Alt-F1,4.

● **SEE ALSO**   Document Summary, Word Count

DOCUMENT SUMMARY

Document Summary lets you store important information about a document so you can easily locate it later. The summary can also be used to help organize your documents.

To Create the Document Summary

1. From the File menu, choose Summary.

2. Choose Extract (Shift-F10) and select Yes to extract summary information from the document.

3. Select each field and type in or edit the information in the text box. Remember to use the scroll bar to display all the fields.

4. If you want to print the summary, choose Print (Shift-F7).

5. When you have finished entering the information, choose OK.

To Modify the Document Summary Setup

You can change the information that is included in the summary.

1. From the File menu, choose Summary.

2. Choose Select Fields (F4).

3. To delete all the fields in one step, choose Clear and answer Yes. You can also highlight any field in the list box on the left to either move it or remove it from the summary, and then choose Move or Remove. If you choose Move, highlight its new location and press ↵.

4. To add fields, highlight any field in the list box on the right and choose Add. Items that are already included are shown with an asterisk.

5. To make the modified summary format the default format for all new documents, select Use as Default (F10).

6. Choose OK or press ↵ until you return to your document.

To Automate the Document Summary

Some items in the document summary can be filled in for you by WordPerfect. For example, if you always indicate the subject of the document in the same way (by using the words "Case Number" or "Subject," for example) WordPerfect can search for that text.

1. From the File menu, choose Summary.

2. Choose Setup (Shift-F1).

3. Select Subject Search Text (1) and type the text in the text box and press ↵. WordPerfect will look for this text in your document and insert the information it finds to the right.

4.   Select **D**efault Descriptive Type (2) and type the kind of document you create most often (letter, memo, report) and press ↵. WordPerfect will always enter this type, but you can edit it in the Document Summary dialog box when you create a different kind of document.

5.   Check **C**reate Summary on Exit/Save (3). WordPerfect will always fill in as many fields as it can automatically; you can complete the summary when you have time.

6.   Choose OK or press ↵ until you return to your document.

● **NOTES**   When you look at the contents of a file in the File Manager, the summary information is the first screen that is displayed. You can also use File Manager's Find capability to search through document summaries. You can always display the summary for the current document by using the Summary command on the File menu.

● **SEE ALSO**   Document Information, File Manager

ENVELOPE

The Envelope command lets you create and print individual envelopes.

To Create an Envelope

Before you select the Envelope command, select the printer you plan to use.

1.   From the Layout menu, choose Envelope (Alt-F12).

2.   Choose **E**nvelope Size (1), select a different envelope size if necessary, and press ↵.

3.   Check **O**mit Return Address (2) if you don't want to print a return address.

4. Check Save Return Address as Default (3) if you want the address you enter to be used each time you print an envelope.

5. If you want to print a return address, select Return Address (4), type the address in the text box, and press F7.

6. If no mailing address is shown in the Mailing Address (5) text box, select it, type the address in the text box, and press F7. If you are creating an envelope for a standard business letter, WordPerfect finds this address and inserts it automatically.

7. To print a Bar Code on the envelope, select POSTNET Bar Code (6) and type the 9- or 11-digit Zip Code in the text box.

8. Choose Print to print it right away or choose Insert to add the envelope to your document; you can save or print it later.

To Define an Envelope

You can create new definitions for envelopes that are not shown in the list.

1. From the Layout menu, choose Envelope (Alt-F12).

2. Choose Setup (Shift-F1).

3. In the Envelope Size (1) list box, highlight an envelope and then choose Create (2).

4. Highlight an item in the Paper Name list box and select Create (2).

5. Type a name for the envelope (for example, you could type "large envelope") and press ↵.

6. In the Paper Type (2) drop-down list box, choose Envelope and press ↵.

7. Select Paper Location (4), if necessary, to change the setting shown. Highlight the correct setting in the list box and choose Select (1). Also, if you do this step, you may need to select Prompt to Load (5).

8. To change the address positions, select **A**djust Text (7) and change the **T**op (1) and/or **S**ide (2) numbers in the text box as needed. Press ↵.

9. When you've made the necessary changes, choose OK to return to the Paper Size/Type dialog box.

10. Press Tab, then ↵ to select Close and return to the Envelope Setup dialog box.

11. Press Tab twice and then ↵ to select OK.

You can now create and print an envelope.

● **NOTES** If your document is not a standard business letter, or if there is more than one address, you can block an address before you choose Envelope and WordPerfect will insert it in the Mailing Address text box.

● **SEE ALSO** Paper Size, Print

EQUATIONS

The Equation Editor lets you create, edit, and format scientific and mathematical equations and insert them in your documents.

To Create an Equation

1. Position the cursor where you want to insert the equation.

2. From the **G**raphics menu, choose Graphics **B**oxes (Alt-F9,1).

3. Choose **C**reate (1).

4. Choose **B**ased on Box Style (Y), highlight Equation Box in the list box, and choose **S**elect (1).

5. If Equation is not selected in the Contents (2) pop-up box, select it now.

6.   Choose Create Equation (3). The Equation Editor, shown in Figure 4, will be displayed.

7.   Enter the equation in the bottom window by typing variables and selecting commands and symbols from the list box. See Table 4 for some sample equations. To select a command or symbol:

- Click on it in the list box and then select the **K**eyword button; or

- Double-click on the command or symbol.

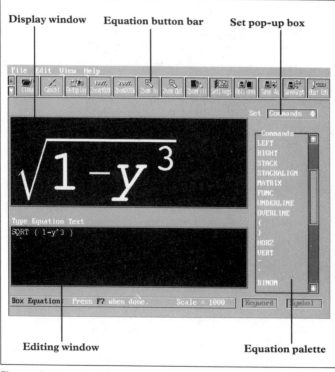

Figure 4: The Equations Editor lets you create and edit equations.

Table 4: Sample Equations Created with the Equations Editor

Equation Text	Result
{a+1} OVER {b–1}	$\dfrac{a+1}{b-1}$
SQRT {1–y^3}	$\sqrt{1-y^3}$
STACK {a–b} # {c–d} # {e–f}	$a-b$ $c-d$ $e-f$

8. From the View menu, choose Redisplay (Ctrl-F3) to make sure the equation is correct. It is displayed in the top window.

9. If you need to edit the equation, press Tab to move to the bottom window or click the bottom window, and then make any changes. Choose Redisplay (Ctrl-F3) again to see how your edits change the equation.

10. When the equation is complete, choose Close (F7) from the File menu and choose OK or press ↵ to return to your document.

You can see the formatted equation by switching to Page Mode (Ctrl-F3,4) or Graphics Mode (Ctrl-F3,3).

To Edit an Equation

You can edit the contents and appearance of an equation at any time.

1. From the Graphics menu, choose Graphics **B**oxes (Alt-F9,1). Or double-click the equation and skip to Step 3 (in Graphics or Page Mode.)

2. Choose Edit (2).

3. Select Counter Number (2) and select Equation Box from the Counter drop-down list box.

4. Type the number in the Number text box and press ↵.

5. Choose Edit Box to display the Edit Graphics Box dialog box.

6. To edit the appearance of the equation, choose any of these options: Options (5), Edit Border/Fill (6), Edit Position (8), Edit Size (9), or Text Flow Around Box (T). Make all the necessary selections in the resulting dialog boxes and choose OK to return to the Edit Graphics Box.

7. To edit the contents of the equation, choose Edit Equation (3).

8. Edit the equation in the bottom window and choose Redisplay (Ctrl-F3) again to see how your edits change the equation.

9. When you finish editing, choose Close (F7) from the File menu and choose OK or ↵ to return to your document

Using the Equation Palettes

The list box on the right of the Equation Editor window displays one of eight Equation Palettes provided by WordPerfect. The palettes display commands, symbols, and other characters frequently used in creating equations. They are grouped in eight categories: Commands, Large, Symbols, Greek, Arrows, Sets, Other, and Functions. You can select items from the palettes to insert in your equations and you can change the palette as needed.

To change the palette:

- Press Tab until Set is selected (has a dotted line), and then press ↵ to open the list box. Press ↓ or ↑ to highlight another palette and press ↵.

- Press and hold the mouse button on the Set pop-up box, drag the mouse to the new palette name, and release the mouse button.

To select an item from a palette:

- Highlight an item and press ↵; or
- Double-click an item.

To Delete an Equation

You can delete an equation in the document window with any of these techniques:

- Position the cursor before the equation and press Delete.

- Click the equation to display the equation box and press Delete (in Graphics and Page Mode only).

- Display the Reveal Codes window and delete the equation code.

● **NOTES** The Equation Editor does not solve equations; it lets you properly format and align them. Equations also can be saved in separate files as text with the File Save As (F10) command or graphics with the File Save As Image command. When saved as graphics files, they can be rotated in your document.

When creating and editing equations in the Equation Editor, files can be retrieved into the editing window. Cut, Copy and Paste are also available.

Table 4 shows some sample equations created in the Equations editor.

● **SEE ALSO** Copy/Copy and Paste, Cut/Cut and Paste/Move, Graphics Boxes, Retrieve

There are several convenient methods for closing documents and exiting WordPerfect.

To Close the Current Document

To close a document it is faster to use Close than Exit because Word-Perfect displays fewer prompts. When closing an unmodified document, the Close command will do it in one step.

To close a document with Close:

1. From the File menu, choose Close. If the document has changed since you last saved it, you'll be prompted to save it. If it has not changed, it will be closed immediately.

2. You can select Yes to save it with the name shown or Save As to save the document with another name.

3. If you choose Save As, enter a name—and, if necessary, the path—in the text box and then choose OK or press ↵.

To close a document with Exit:

1. From the File menu, choose Exit (F7). You'll always be prompted to save your document, whether or not it has been modified.

2. You can select Yes to save it with the name shown or Save As to save the document with another name.

3. If you choose Save As, enter a name—and, if necessary, the path—in the text box and then choose OK or press ↵.

4. Choose Yes at the prompt to close the document if more than one document is open. Or, choose Yes at the prompt to exit WordPerfect if only the current document is open.

When displaying multiple windows with Close boxes, you can also click the upper-left corner of a document window to close the window and document in one step.

To Exit WordPerfect

When you exit WordPerfect, you'll always be prompted to save any open and modified documents.

1. From the File menu, choose Exit WP (Home, F7). You'll be prompted to save all open documents. They are listed in the dialog box.

2. You can check Save next to each document you want to save. Modified documents are shown with the Save box already checked.

3. Choose Save and Exit.

● **NOTES**   You can cancel the closing or exiting operation at any time by choosing the Cancel button or pressing Esc. Any open documents remain open.

● **SEE ALSO**   Cancel, Save/Save As, Windows

N E W

FAX SERVICES

If you have an internal fax/modem, you can fax a WordPerfect document with WordPerfect's Print, Fax Services command. You must have already installed a fax program on your computer in order to use WordPerfect's Fax Services feature. The options provided by Fax Services are limited to those available through your fax program and may vary slightly from those described here.

To Send the Current Document

1. From the File menu, choose Print-Fax (Shift-F7).

2. Choose Fax Services (9).

3. To tell WordPerfect where to send the fax:

    • Select and mark the Phonebook Entries by highlighting each and pressing the asterisk key, spacebar, or 1. Then choose Send Fax.

    • Choose Manual Dial, enter the information in the text boxes, and choose OK.

4. Choose Send Fax.

5.   Select and change any Fax Options (see "Fax Options").

To Send a Document on-Disk

You can resend files that have been sent previously and files that have been saved with the Save as an image for Fax on Disk option (see "Notes"). These files will have a .FAX extension. To send a document on-disk:

1.   From the File menu, choose Print-Fax (Shift-F7).

2.   Choose Fax Services (9).

3.   To tell WordPerfect where to send the fax:

   • Select and mark the Phonebook Entries by highlighting each and pressing the asterisk key, spacebar, or 1. Then choose Send Fax.

   • Choose Manual Dial (2), enter the information in the text boxes, and choose OK.

4.   Choose Fax on Disk (6).

5.   In the Send Files dialog box, enter the file name in the text box and press ↵. The file name will appear in the Files to Send list box. To enter additional files to send, choose Filename (1) and enter the next file to be sent.

6.   Choose Send File to send the fax.

Fax Options

The following settings and options are available in the Send Fax dialog box.

Full Document (1)	Faxes the current document.
Page (2)	Faxes the current page.
Document on-Disk (3)	Sends the document on-disk.
Multiple Pages (4)	Opens a dialog box where you can select the pages to fax.
Blocked Text (5)	Faxes the currently selected (blocked) text.

Fax on Disk (6)	Opens a dialog box where you can enter the name of the fax image file. You can fax any document on the hard disk or a floppy disk if they have been previously saved with the Save as an Image for Fax on Disk option.
Save as an image for Fax on Disk (7)	Saves the document as a fax file so it can be resent with the Fax on Disk option in the future. You enter the file name in the text box; fax files are saved with a .FAX extension.
Coversheet (8)	Lets you create a coversheet for your fax.
Send Time (9)	Lets you enter the date and time when you want the fax to be sent, if you do not want it sent immediately.
Resolution	Determines the resolution and print quality with which you want the document faxed.
Priority, Routing, Billing	Lets you prioritize the fax and decide the line on which it will be sent and the billing procedure.

● **NOTES**   To cancel a fax in progress, choose Print-Fax from the File menu (Shift-F7), Fax Services (9), Fax Activity (4), and Cancel Current Fax (1).

Some fax boards are capable of binary file transfer, which means they can send and receive images that have not been previously saved as an image for the purpose of faxing.

● **SEE ALSO**   Print

FILE MANAGER

File Manager provides many commands to help you manage files and navigate directories.

To Specify the Directory

When you first open File Manager, you'll want to specify the directory to display.

1. From the File menu, choose File Manager (F5).

2. In the Directory text box, type or edit the name of the Directory whose contents you want to display and choose OK or press ↵.

If you want to change the default directory for the current session, press the equals (=) key before you type the directory name.

File Manager opens with the contents of the directory you selected shown in the list box. Subdirectories are listed first, followed by files.

To Navigate the Directory Tree

You can also use the Directory Tree feature to see a graphic representation of all the directories on the current drive.

1. From the File menu, choose File Manager (F5).

2. Choose Directory Tree (F8).

3. If the directory you want to display is on another drive, choose Other Drive (2), highlight a drive in the list, and choose Select or double-click the drive.

4. Highlight a directory on the tree and choose Select Directory (1) or double-click the directory.

File Manager Options

Once File Manager is displayed, you can use any of the options on the right to manipulate files. Highlight a single file or mark and unmark several files by highlighting each and pressing the asterisk (*) key or spacebar.

Option	Description
Open into new document (1)	Opens the highlighted file or up to nine marked files in new document windows.
Retrieve into current document (2)	Retrieves the highlighted file into the current document.
Look (3)	Displays the document summary and contents of a file in a view window (you can't edit the file).
Copy (4)	Copies the highlighted or marked files to a directory you specify, or to the current directory if you specify a different file name.
Move/Rename (5)	Moves the highlighted or marked files to a directory you specify, or lets you rename by specifying a different file name. You can also move and rename in one step by entering both a new destination and file name, or file name with wildcards if you are moving and renaming groups of marked files.
Delete (6)	Deletes the highlighted or marked files.
Print (7)	Prints the contents of the highlighted or marked files.
Print List (8)	Prints a list of all files in the File Manager list box.
Sort by (9)	Changes the way files are organized and displayed in the File Manager list box.

Option	Description
Change Default Dir (H)	Changes the default directory for the current WordPerfect session and also lets you create a new directory by entering it in the text box.
Current Dir (F5)	Changes the directory whose contents are displayed in the File Manager list box.
Find (F)	Searches for a text string you specify. You may use wild cards (* and ?) in your search.
Search (F2)	Searches for a file name you specify. You may use wild cards (* and ?) in your search.
Name Search (N)	Moves the cursor to a file or directory as you begin to type its name. To move to a file, begin typing the file name. To move to a directory, begin by typing a backslash (\) before typing the file name.

● **SEE ALSO**   Document Summary, Open, Print, QuickList, Retrieve

FONT

You can select a font to be used for all documents, the current document, or specific text within a document. The available fonts are based on the printer you have selected.

To Set the Initial Document Font

1.   From the Layout menu, choose **D**ocument (Shift-F8,4).

2.   Choose Initial Font (3).

3.   Select the font (typeface) you want from the Font (1) drop-down list box and press ↵.

4.   Select the point size you want from the Size (2) drop-down list box and press ↵.

5.   Select whether to apply the font change to the Current Document Only (3) or All New Documents (4).

6.   Choose OK or press ↵.

7.   Press ↵ or choose OK again.

To Change the Font within a Document

1.   If you haven't yet typed the text, position the cursor where you want to begin changing the font. If you've already entered the text, select (block) the text you want to modify.

2.   From the Font menu, choose Font (Ctrl-F8).

3.   Select the font (typeface) you want from the Font (1) drop-down list box and press ↵.

4.   Select the point size you want from the Size (2) drop-down list box and press ↵.

5.   Choose OK or press ↵.

To Change the Font Using the Ribbon

With the Ribbon displayed, you can quickly change the font using the Font and Size drop-down list boxes.

1.   If you haven't yet typed the text, position the cursor where you want to begin changing the font. If you've already entered the text, select (block) the text you want to modify.

2.   Click on the Font drop-down list button and double-click on one of the fonts in the list to select a different font. If necessary, use the scroll buttons to scroll through the available fonts in the list.

3. Click on the Size drop-down list button, and double-click on one of the sizes in the list. If necessary, use the scroll buttons to scroll through the available sizes in the list.

● **NOTES** If you change the selected printer for a document after you've selected fonts you may see an asterisk (*) in the font code (in the Reveal Codes window). The asterisk means that the font is not available on the newly selected printer, so WordPerfect has substituted another font.

● **SEE ALSO** Codes, Font Attributes, Printer Select, Reveal Codes, Ribbon

FONT ATTRIBUTES

You can change the appearance, relative size, and position of the selected font by changing its attributes.

To Change One Attribute

1. If you haven't yet typed the text, position the cursor where you want to begin changing the font. If you've already entered the text, select (block) the text you want to modify.

2. From the Font menu, choose any attribute you want to add: Size/Position, **Bold**, Underline, **D**ouble Underline, Italics, Outline, Shadow, Small Caps, **R**edline, or Strikeout.

To Change Several Attributes

1. If you haven't yet typed the text, position the cursor where you want to begin changing the font. If you've already entered the text, select (block) the text you want to modify.

2. From the Font menu, choose Font (Ctrl-F8).

3. Select options in the **A**ppearance (3), **R**elative Size (4),
Position (5), and **U**nderline (6) group boxes. You can check
more than one attribute under each option.

4. Choose OK or press ⏎.

The available options under each attribute are:

Attribute	Options
Appearance (3)	Bold, Underline, Dbl Underline, Italics, Outline, Shadow, Small Caps, Redline, Strikeout
Relative Size (4)	Normal, Fine, Small, Large, Very Large, Extra Large
Position (5)	Normal, Superscript, Subscript
Underline (6)	Spaces, Tabs

To Return to the Original Attributes

To return to the original font after you finish typing in text, choose
Normal from the **F**ont menu.

● **NOTES**   You can quickly delete an attribute by deleting its
code. To delete all attributes assigned to the text, select the text and
choose Normal from the Font menu.

● **SEE ALSO**   Codes, Font, Reveal Codes

FOOTNOTES
AND ENDNOTES

Use Footnotes to provide additional information or references at
the bottom of each page. Use Endnotes to place references at the
end of the document.

To Create a Footnote or Endnote

1. From the Layout menu, choose Footnote (Ctrl-F7,1) or Endnote (Ctrl-F7,3).

2. Choose Create (1).

3. Type the text of the note. You can also paste the text of the note if you've cut or copied it to the buffer, or retrieve a file that contains the note instead of typing the text.

4. From the File menu, choose Exit (F7) to close this window.

You can see the note by switching to Page mode (Ctrl-F3,4) or Print Preview (Shift-F7,7).

To Edit a Footnote or Endnote

1. From the Layout menu, choose Footnote (Ctrl-F7,1) or Endnote (Ctrl-F7,3).

2. Choose Edit (2).

3. Type the number of the note you want to edit and choose OK or press ↵.

4. Edit the text. All WordPerfect editing keys are available.

5. From the File menu, choose Exit (F7) to close this window.

To Renumber Notes

When you add or delete a note, WordPerfect automatically renumbers the notes for you. However, if your document is stored in several files, you'll need to renumber the first note in each file to be sure that all the notes are numbered in sequence.

1. Position the cursor where you want to begin renumbering.

2. From the Layout menu, choose Footnote (Ctrl-F7,1) or Endnote (Ctrl-F7,3).

3. Choose Number (3).

4. Select New Number (1). Type the new number in the text box and press ↵.

5. You can also change the Numbering Method (2) by selecting a different method from the drop-down list box and
pressing ↵. If you select Characters, type a character in the
Character (6) text box. You may use WordPerfect characters.

6. Choose OK or press ↵. If you used (Ctrl-F7, 1), you also
need to select OK.

To Delete a Note

Use either of these techniques to delete a note:

• Position the cursor before the note number and press
Delete.

• Display the Reveal Codes window and delete the code.

● **NOTES**   The Footnote and Endnote Options dialog boxes
present a number of formatting options for notes. You can also
change the style, font, or attributes of individual or all notes.

● **SEE ALSO**   Cut/Cut and Paste/Move, Delete, Font, Font Attributes, Reveal Codes, Styles, WP Characters

GO TO

With the Go To command, you can quickly move the cursor
anywhere in the document.

To Move to a Page or Location

1. From the Edit menu, choose Go To (Ctrl-Home).

2. Type a page number and press ↵. To move to a specific
location, use any of the keys shown in Table 5.

Table 5: Go To Keys

Keys	Moves the Cursor to
Any character except numbers	The next occurrence of the character. The operation is case-sensitive.
↵	The next hard return.
↑	The top of the page or column.
↓	The bottom of the page or column.
Alt-F4	The beginning of the blocked text. Also unblocks it.
Ctrl-Home	The previous cursor position.
→	In a table or column format, one column to the right.
←	In a table or column format, one column to the left.
Home-←	In a table or column format, the first column.
Home-→	In a table or column format, the last column.
Cell Name	When editing the table structure, the cell with that name. After you type the cell name you must press ↵.

GO TO SHELL

The Go To Shell command lets you execute DOS commands without exiting WordPerfect.

To Execute DOS
Commands from WordPerfect

To quickly execute a single command:

1. From the File menu, choose Go To Shell (Ctrl-F1).

2. Choose DOS Command (6), type the command you want to execute, and press ↵.

3. Press ↵ to return to your document.

To execute more than one command:

1. From the File menu, choose Go To Shell (Ctrl-F1).

2. Choose Go to DOS (1) and enter the commands as you normally would.

3. When you are finished, type EXIT and press ↵ to return to your document.

● **NOTES**　If you are running WordPerfect Shell 4.0, you can also use the command to switch to another active program and to send mail. Go To Shell also lets you save information to and retrieve information from the Clipboard.

● **See Also**　Append

Grammatik is a WordPerfect utility that provides complete and thorough grammar, spelling, and style checking. Grammatik analyzes your document interactively and helps you correct any errors it finds.

To Check and Edit a File

1. From the Tools menu, choose Writing Tools (Alt-F1).

2. Choose Grammatik (3) to display the Grammatik window.

3. Press I to begin an Interactive check of the current document.

The Grammatik window is displayed, similar to that in Figure 5. The first possible error is highlighted in the top half of the screen. Advice for correcting the problem is shown in the bottom half.

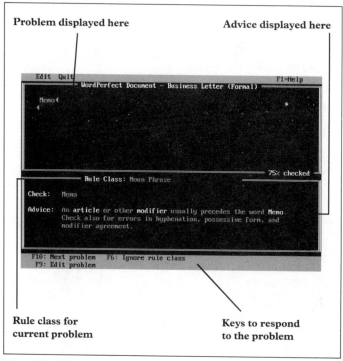

Figure 5: The Grammatik window

4. Press F9 to edit the document. The cursor is in the top half of the window on the error.

5. Edit the item and press F10 to have Grammatik continue checking.

6. Repeat steps 4 and 5 until you finish checking the document.

You can also use the commands on the Edit menu and function keys shown at the bottom of the screen to respond to Grammatik's error prompts. The main Grammatik screen is displayed when the document has been completely checked.

To Search the Entire File for Errors

Instead of editing in interactive mode, you can have Grammatik search and mark the entire file.

1. From the Tools menu, choose Writing Tools (Alt-F1).

2. Choose Grammatik (3) to display the Grammatik window.

3. From the Checking menu, choose Mark to mark all the errors found in the current document.

4. Choose Quit from the File menu or just press Q to return to your WordPerfect document window. The errors are marked in your document.

Once you've reviewed the errors, return to Grammatik to unmark the file.

1. From the Tools menu, choose Writing Tools (Alt-F1).

2. Choose Grammatik to display the Grammatik (3) window.

3. From the Checking menu, choose Unmark.

4. Choose Quit from the File menu or just press Q.

To Select a Writing Style

Grammatik checks each document based on a selected writing style. Before you begin checking a particular document, you may want to change the writing style.

1. From the Grammatik **P**references menu, choose **W**riting Style.

2. Highlight a style in the list box and press ↵ or double-click it.

To View Statistics

Grammatik collects and analyzes information about your document to help you determine its readability.

1. From the Statistics menu, choose Show Statistics.

2. After you read the first screen, press ↵ to see an interpretation of the statistics.

3. When you are finished, press Esc.

● **NOTES**   Once you display the Grammatik window, you can open another document to check by choosing Open from the File menu. Highlight a file name in the list box and press ↵ or double-click a file name.

When you have finished using Grammatik, choose Quit from the File menu or just press Q to return to your WordPerfect document window.

● **SEE ALSO**   Speller

GRAPHICS BOXES

Graphics boxes can be used to insert graphics, such as drawings, images, clip art and charts, in a document. They also make it possible to insert equations, tables, text, and sidebars.

To Create a Graphics Box

1. Position the cursor where you want to insert the graphics box.

2. From the Graphics menu, choose Graphics Boxes (Alt-F9,1).

3. Choose Create (1).

4. Choose Based on Box Style (Y), highlight Figure Box in the list box in order to insert a graphic, and choose Select (1).

See "Graphics Box Styles" for an explanation of the styles. Make sure that Image or Image on Disk is selected in the Contents (2) pop-up box. See "Notes" for more information.

5. Select Filename (1) to select the graphics file to insert in the box.

6. Type a file name in the text box or use the File List (F5) button to display a list of files, and then select a file.

7. Choose OK or press ↵.

8. Choose Create Caption (4) if you want to add a caption to the graphic. The Caption Editor will be displayed.

9. Enter the caption and choose Close (F7) to return to the Create Graphics Box dialog box.

10. Choose OK or press ↵ to return to the document window.

You can edit the image inside the box with the Image Editor.

To Modify a Graphics Box

You can edit the appearance of a graphics box or the caption at any time. These steps also show you how to add a caption to an existing graphics box.

1. From the Graphics menu, choose Graphics Boxes (Alt-F9,1).

2. Choose Edit (2).

3. Select Counter Number (2), select Figure Box from the Counter drop-down list box, type the number in the Number text box, and press ↵.

4. Choose Edit Box to display the Edit Graphics Box dialog box.

5. To add a caption, choose Create Caption (4). To edit the existing caption, choose Edit Caption (4). Add or edit the text in the window and press F7 to close the Caption Editor.

6. To edit the appearance of the box, choose any of these options: Options (5), Edit Border/Fill (6), Attach To (7), Edit Position (8), Edit Size (9), or Text Flow Around Box (T). Make all the necessary selections in the resulting dialog boxes and choose OK to return to the Edit Graphics Box dialog box.

7. When you finish editing, choose OK to return to your document.

If you're working in Page or Graphics mode, you can open the Edit Graphics Box dialog box in one step by double-clicking the box.

You can also resize a graphics box by selecting it and dragging its handles (the small black squares) in or out.

To Delete a Graphics Box

You can delete a graphics box in the document window with either of these techniques:

- In Graphics or Page mode, click the graphic to display the surrounding box and press Delete.

- Display the Reveal Codes window and delete the box code.

Graphics Box Styles

Eight graphics box styles are available, each with a different look and purpose. However, you can actually use any box style and then modify the border, fill, corner, and line color to achieve the results you want. Table 6 explains what the different styles are.

Table 6: Graphics Box Styles

Style Name	Recommended Use
Figure Box	Drawings and other graphics created in a WordPerfect-compatible graphic format, clip art, and charts.
Table Box	Spreadsheets, statistical tables, and text tables.
Text Box	Sidebars and other text you want to treat differently or highlight within the document.
User Box	Drawings, clip art, charts, tables, equations, and text that you want to place an invisible border around.
Equation Box	Mathematical and scientific equations that will appear on their own line.
Button Box	Drawings, clip art, icons, and text that you want to give a three-dimensional "button" appearance to.
Watermark Image Box	Drawings, clip art, icons, and logos that you want to place behind the text on a page.
Inline Equation Box	Mathematical and scientific equations that will appear within a line of text.

● **NOTES**   If the image is large enough that it might significantly increase the size of your document, or if you intend to edit the graphics file outside of WordPerfect, you should change the Contents from Image to Image on Disk in the Edit Graphics Box dialog box before selecting the image file.

If you use Attach To to attach the graphics box to a page, paragraph, or character, the box and its contents move with the text when you edit your document. You can also move a graphics box by selecting it and dragging it with the mouse.

● **SEE ALSO** Borders, Equations, Graphics Retrieve, Image Editor, Move, Tables, Watermark

GRAPHICS LINES

The Graphics Lines feature places horizontal and vertical lines anywhere in your document.

To Create a Line

1. Position the cursor where you want to insert the line.

2. From the Graphics menu, choose Graphics Lines (Alt-F9,2).

3. Choose Create (1).

4. Select the Line Orientation (1), either Horizontal or Vertical.

5. Select the Horizontal Position (2) of the line. Use Set to specify the distance from the left edge of the page, enter the distance in the text box, and press ↵.

6. Select the Vertical Position (3) of the line. Use Set to specify the distance from the top edge of the page, enter the distance in the text box, and press ↵.

7. Select Length (5), enter the line length, and press ↵.

8. Choose Line Style (6), select the style in the list box, and choose Select (1).

9. Choose OK or press ↵.

To Edit a Line

1. From the Graphics menu, choose Graphics Lines (Alt-F9,2).

2. Choose Edit (2).

3. Select Graphics Line Number (1), type the number in the text box, and press ↵.

4.   Choose Edit Line to display the Edit Graphics Line dialog box.

5.   Make any changes in the dialog box and choose OK or press ↵ when you are done.

If you're working in Page or Graphics mode, you can open the Edit Graphics Line dialog box in one step by double-clicking the line.

To Delete a Line

You can delete a line in the document window with either of these techniques.

- In Page or Graphics mode, click the line to display the surrounding box and press Delete.

- Display the Reveal Codes window and delete the line code.

● **NOTES**   In Graphics mode, you can also move and resize a line in the document window by using the mouse. Click the line to display the surrounding box and drag the line to reposition it. Drag the handles (the small black squares at the middle and each end) to change the line's length and width.

The Edit Graphics Line dialog box also lets you change the Line Thickness, Color, and Spacing.

● **SEE ALSO**   Line Draw, Move

When you work in Graphics mode WordPerfect displays, as best it can, the body of your document—both the text and graphics—as it will look when printed. To do this, WordPerfect attempts to match the fonts and attributes with the available display attributes.

To Work in Graphics Mode

Graphics mode has a check on the menu when active. To select it, choose Graphics Mode (Ctrl-F3,3) from the View menu. Figure 6 shows the main elements of the document window that can be displayed when Graphics mode is active.

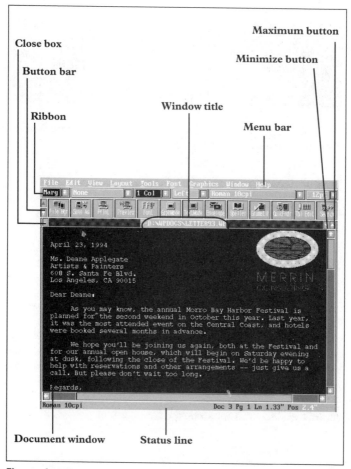

Figure 6: The Graphics mode window

● **NOTES**   WordPerfect displays graphics in color even if you have not selected a color printer. In Graphics mode, headers, footers, footnotes, and endnotes are not displayed. Use Page mode if you want to display them.

● **SEE ALSO**   Page Mode, Text Mode

N E W

GRAPHICS RETRIEVE

You can retrieve a graphic directly into your document with the Retrieve Image command.

To Retrieve a Graphics File

1. Position the cursor where you want to insert the graphic.

2. From the Graphics menu, choose Retrieve Image.

3. Type a file name in the text box or select the File List (F5) button and then press ↵ or select OK to display a list of files.

4. Highlight the name of the file in the list box and choose Select (1).

● **NOTES**   You can retrieve clip art, charts, or drawings with this method. WordPerfect automatically places the image in a figure box and applies the default style for the box.

● **SEE ALSO**   Graphics Boxes, Image Editor

HEADERS AND FOOTERS

You can add multiple headers and footers to a document.

To Create a Header or Footer

1. Position the cursor anywhere on the page where you want to insert a header or a footer.

2. Choose Header/Footer/Watermark from the Layout menu.

3. Choose Headers (1) or Footers (2), depending on what you want to add to your document. Then choose Header/Footer **A** or **B**, depending on which one you want to create.

4. Select whether to show the header on **A**ll Pages (1), **E**ven Pages (2), or **O**dd (3) Pages, and choose **C**reate.

5. Type the text of the header or footer. WordPerfect's editing keys and commands are available in this window.

6. From the File menu, choose Exit (F7) to close this window.

7. Repeat steps 3 through 6 to create another header or footer. When you are done, choose OK or press ↵ to return to the document window.

You can see the headers and footers by switching to Page mode (Ctrl-F3,4) or Print Preview (Shift-F7,7).

To Edit a Header or Footer

1. Choose Header/Footer/Watermark from the Layout menu.

2. To adjust the space between the header or footer and the body of the document, select either **H**eaders (1) and **S**pace Below Header (3) or **F**ooters (2) and **S**pace Above Footer (3), type a measurement in the text box, and press ↵.

3. To turn off the header or footer, select **H**eaders (1) or **F**ooters (2), and then Header/Footer **A** or **B**, and choose Off.

4. To edit the contents, choose the header or footer you want to edit and choose **E**dit.

5. Edit the header or footer.

6. From the File menu, choose Exit (F7) to return to the document window.

To Delete a Header or Footer

To delete a header or footer, position the cursor at the beginning of the document, display the Reveal Codes window, and delete the code. If you have multiple headers, you can first position the cursor on the code to read its contents before deleting the code.

● **NOTES**   You can include up to two headers and two footers on any page in your document. WordPerfect labels them as Header A and B and Footer A and B in order to keep track of them, but the letters have no significance. You can change a header or footer within your document by turning it off and creating a new one.

You can suppress a header or footer on one or more pages by using the Page command on the Layout menu. The Page command also lets you add a page number to the header or footer. Use the Date command on the Tools menu to add a date code.

● **SEE ALSO**   Date and Time, Delete, Page Format, Print Preview, Reveal Codes, Watermarks

HELP

WordPerfect's on-line help feature provides context-sensitive information, an indexed reference of commands and features, and steps to perform common tasks.

To Display Context-Sensitive Help

- Press F1 if you are using the default keyboard layout.
- Press F3 if you have selected the CUA keyboard layout.

To Search for a Topic

1. From the Help menu, choose Index.

2. Press ↓ to place the highlight bar on a topic in the list or scroll with the mouse and click a topic. Or, choose Name Search and begin to type the topic. WordPerfect moves the highlight bar and highlights the closest match as you type.

3. When the topic is highlighted, choose Look.

● **NOTES**   All the help options are available by choosing Contents (F1) from the Help menu and at the bottom of the Help window. When you are finished using on-line help, choose Cancel to close the Help window or press the Esc key.

Hypertext lets you create a link or "jump" in one document to a bookmark in the same or another document. It also lets you run a macro by selecting marked text within the document. The bookmark or macro must be created before you create the hypertext link.

To Create a Hypertext Link

1. Select (block) the text that will become the hypertext.

2. From the Tools menu, choose Hypertext (Alt-F5,6).

3. Choose Create Link (1).

4.   From here you can link to a bookmark in the current or in another document, or run a macro:

- To link to a bookmark in the current document, select Go to **B**ookmark (1). Choose List Bookmarks (F5), highlight a bookmark in the list box, and choose Select.

- To link to a bookmark in another document, first select Go to **O**ther Document (2) and enter the document path and name. Next, place the cursor in the Bookmark text box below. Choose List Bookmarks (F5), highlight a bookmark in the list box, and choose Select or press ⏎.

- To run a macro, select Run **M**acro (3). Choose List Macros, highlight a macro in the list box, and choose Select (1).

5.   Choose either **H**ighlighted Text (4) or **B**utton (5) in the Hypertext Appearance group box.

6.   Choose OK or press ⏎.

You cannot view a hypertext button in Text mode; switch to Page mode (Ctrl-F3,4) or Graphics mode (Ctrl-F3,3) to view it.

To Edit a Hypertext Link

1.   Position the cursor on the hypertext.

2.   From the **T**ools menu, choose **H**ypertext (Alt-F5,6).

3.   Choose Edit Hypertext **S**tyle (8) to edit the appearance of the link displayed as highlighted text. Delete or add font attributes and press F7 to close this window.

4.   Choose Edit **L**ink (2) to edit the contents of the link.

5.   Make any changes in the dialog box and choose OK or press ⏎.

To Use Hypertext Links

To use the hypertext links you create, they must be active.

1.   From the **T**ools menu, choose **H**ypertext (Alt-F5,6).

2.   Check Hypertext is **A**ctive (9).

3.   Choose OK or press ↵.

To then select a hypertext link:

• Double-click the hypertext.

• Position the cursor on the hypertext and press ↵.

To activate a single hypertext link without first checking the Hypertext is Active option:

1.   Position the cursor on the hypertext.

2.   From the **T**ools menu, choose **H**ypertext (Alt-F5,6).

3.   Select **J**ump/Run (4). You will be prompted to save the document if it has not already been saved.

To Delete a Hypertext Link

1.   Position the cursor on the hypertext.

2.   From the **T**ools menu, choose **H**ypertext (Alt-F5,6).

3.   Select **D**elete Link(s) (3).

Or, display the Reveal Codes window and delete the code.

• **NOTES**   While hypertext is active, ↵ activates the link, Tab moves the cursor to the next link, and Shift-Tab moves the cursor to the previous link. Remove the check from the Hypertext is Active check box to make ↵ and Tab function normally.

Symbols can also be turned into hypertext.

• **SEE ALSO**   Bookmark, Font Attributes, Graphics Mode, Macros, Page Mode, Reveal Codes

HYPHENATION

You can create a hyphenation zone at the right margin in order to have WordPerfect hyphenate words that won't fit on the line.

To Turn Hyphenation On or Off

You can hyphenate only part of a document by turning the hyphenation on and off as needed.

1. Position the cursor where you want to turn hyphenation on or off.

2. From the Layout menu, choose Line (Shift-F8,1).

3. Check Hyphenation (6) to turn it on. Remove the check to turn it off.

4. Choose OK or press ↵. If you used (Shift-F8,1), you'll also need to select Close or press ↵ a second time.

If Hyphenation is currently set to prompt (the default is When Required), WordPerfect will prompt you as it begins to hyphenate. See "Hyphenation Options" for a description of the possible responses.

To Define the Hyphenation Zone

1. Position the cursor where you want to begin the changed hyphenation zone.

2. From the Layout menu, choose Line (Shift-F8,1).

3. Select Hyphenation Zone (7) and type new numbers in the Left and Right text boxes. Press ↵ after each option. Higher numbers result in fewer hyphenated words, and lower numbers result in more hyphenated words.

4. Choose OK or press ↵. If you used (Shift-F8,1), you'll also need to select Close or press ↵ a second time.

The hyphenation zone is calculated based on the line length. The Left value determines where it begins; the right value determines

how far it extends past the right margin. For example, if a line is 6.0 inches and the Left value is set to 10 percent, the hyphenation zone begins 0.6 inches to the left of the right margin. If the Right value for that line is 5 percent, the hyphenation zone ends 0.3 inches after the right margin.

To Set the Hyphenation Method

To select the method WordPerfect will use to prompt you when hyphenating:

1. From the File menu, choose Setup (Shift-F1).

2. Choose Environment (3).

3. Select Prompt for Hyphenation (6), and select Never, Always or When Required.

4. Choose OK or press ↵ twice. If you used Shift-F1, press ↵ to choose Close.

Hyphenation Options

WordPerfect displays these hyphenation options when it prompts you:

Insert Hyphen (1)	A hyphen is inserted in the word as shown.
Insert Space (2)	A space is inserted in the word instead of a hyphen.
Hyphenation SRt (3)	The word is divided with a soft return instead of a hyphen.
Suspend Hyphenation (4)	Hyphenation is turned off temporarily during a process such as scrolling a document.
Ignore Word (5)	The entire word is placed on the next line and WordPerfect does not try to hyphenate it again if it appears later in the document.

• **NOTES**   WordPerfect uses the speller file to determine where
to hyphenate words. However, you can override WordPerfect's
hyphenation of a particular word by inserting a soft hyphen (press
Ctrl-Shift-hyphen) in it. This way, the word is only hyphenated if it
falls in the hyphenation zone.

• **SEE ALSO**   Setup, Speller

The Image Editor lets you scale, crop, rotate, and modify the color
and fill of many graphic images.

To Edit an Image

You can edit an image once it has been retrieved into a graphics box.

1.   From the Graphics menu, choose Graphics **B**oxes
(Alt-F9,1). Or, double-click on the image (in Graphics or
Page mode) and skip to step 5.

2.   Choose Edit (2).

3.   Select **C**ounter Number (2) and select Figure Box from the
Counter drop-down list box. Type the number in the Number text box and press ↵.

4.   Choose Edit Box to display the Edit Graphics Box dialog box.

5.   Choose Image Editor (3). The Image Editor, as shown in
Figure 7, is displayed. Use any of the options to edit the
image.

6.   When you are finished editing, choose Close (F7), then
choose OK or press ↵.

Image Editor button bar   Editing window

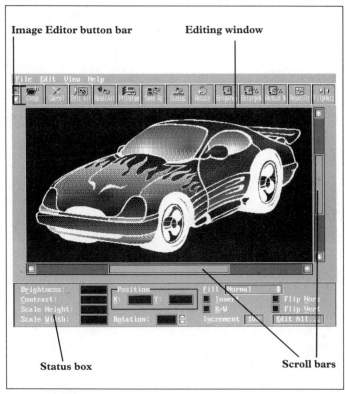

Status box   Scroll bars

Figure 7: The Image Editor window

Image Editor Options

You can select edit options from the status box at the bottom of the Image Editor window, from the Edit menu, and from the button bar. If you intend to make many changes to the image, choose Edit All from the Edit menu or the Edit All option in the lower-right corner of the button bar to display all the options. The following chart summarizes the options in the Edit All dialog box.

Attributes (1)

Flip Horizontal flips the image on its horizontal axis. Flip Vertical flips the image on its vertical axis. Invert Color changes the colors to their complements. Show Background toggles background shading and fills on and off. Black and White converts a color image to black and white, without shades of gray. When converting a black and white image, enter a number between 1 and 255 for the B/W Threshold. Gray values below the number you enter are converted to white, gray values above are converted to black.

Color Adjust (2)

Enter a number between −1.0 (all black) and 1.0 (all white) in the Brightness text box to darken or lighten the image. Enter a number between −1.0 (minimum contrast) and 1.0 (maximum contrast) in the Contrast text box to modify the image contrast.

Position (3)

Enter a number in the Horizontal and Vertical text boxes to move the image around inside the graphics box. A negative Horizontal number moves the image to the left; a positive number moves the image to the right. A negative Vertical number moves the image down; a positive number moves the image up. Enter a number in the Scale Width and Scale Height text boxes to specify a width and height. A number less than 1.0 decreases the image size; greater than 1.0 increases its size. In the Rotation box, specify the degree of rotation from 0 to 359.

| Fill (4) | Choose Transparent to change the image to a transparent outline. Choose White to change the image to a nontransparent outline. |
| Print Parameters (5) | Set the Dither Method, Dither Source, and Halftone options in the Print Parameters dialog box. |

● **SEE ALSO**   Graphics Boxes, Graphics Retrieve

INDENT

Indent moves an entire paragraph the equivalent of one tab stop.

To Indent a Paragraph

1.   Position the cursor at the beginning of the paragraph to be indented.

2.   From the Layout menu, choose **A**lignment.

3.   Choose the type of indenting you want to apply to the paragraph:

Indent → (F4)	Inserts a left indent, which moves the paragraph to the right of the left margin.
Indent →← (Shift-F4)	Inserts a double indent, which indents the paragraph from both the right and left margins.
Hanging Indent	Inserts a hanging indent, which moves every line of the paragraph except the first to the right of the left margin.

- **NOTES**   You can insert the indent either before or after you enter text. The size of the indent is based on the size of the current tab settings. You can insert more than one left indent or double indent at the beginning of a paragraph in order to increase the size of the indentation.

To delete the indent, display the Reveal Codes window and delete the indent code.

- **SEE ALSO**   Margins, Tabs

INDEX

WordPerfect can automatically generate an index that includes headings and subheadings, using both the entries you mark manually and a list of entries (called a concordance file).

To Mark Index Entries

1. Select (block) the text you want to insert as an entry in the index.

2. From the Tools menu, choose Index and then choose Mark (Alt-F5,4,1). The selected text is shown in the Mark Index text box. You can edit this text if you want the index entry to read differently. For example, if the selected text is *books* but you want it to appear under the heading *Book*, edit it in the text box.

3. To mark it as a heading only, choose OK. You can also include a subheading for the entry or mark the text as a subheading.

   - To include a subheading for the entry, type it in the Subheading (2) text box and choose OK.

   - To mark it as a subheading, type a heading in the Heading (1) text box, press ↵, and select Subheading. WordPerfect moves the originally blocked text to the

Subheading box automatically. Choose OK or press ↵
to close this dialog box.

Repeat the steps to mark each index entry. When you are finished,
define the index or create a concordance file if you want to use one
when you generate the index.

To Create a Concordance File

A concordance file is a document you create in WordPerfect that
lists all the words and phrases you want included in your index.
Once you create a concordance file, WordPerfect can search your
document for each item in the list and automatically mark it to be
included in the index.

You can use a concordance file exclusively instead of marking individual index entries, or you can use a concordance file and also
manually mark some individual entries in your document. Word-
Perfect can generate the index using both methods.

1. From the File menu, choose New.

2. Type each word or phrase that you want to include. After
    each entry, press ↵.

You can also use Copy and Paste on the Edit menu to copy entries from
your document to the concordance file instead of retyping them.

3. Alphabetize the list by using the Sort command on the
    Tools menu. WordPerfect will be able to generate the
    index faster if it is alphabetized.

4. From the File menu, choose Save. Enter a file name and
    choose OK or press ↵. Make a note of the name, as you
    will need to enter it when you define the index.

When you are finished, follow the steps to define the index.

To Define the Index

You can define the location for the index and the numbering format.

1. Position the cursor at the end of the document or at an
    alternate location where you want the index to appear.

2.   To begin the index on a new page, enter a page break by pressing Ctrl-↵.

3.   Type **Index** and press ↵.

4.   From the **T**ools menu, choose Index and then choose Define (Alt-F5,2,4).

5.   Select a Numbering mode from the following options:

None (1)	No page numbers are included with the index entries.
# **F**ollows Entry (2)	The page numbers are placed after the entries.
(#) Follows Entry (3)	The page numbers are placed in parentheses after the entries.
# Flush **R**ight (4)	The page numbers are right-justified.
…# Flush Right (5)	The page numbers are right-justified and preceded by a dot leader.

6.   Select Co**m**bine Sequential Page Numbers (7) so that each sequential page number will not be printed out.

7.   If you have created a concordance file, select Concordance File and enter the file name in the text box.

8.   Choose OK or press ↵.

You can also modify the index level styles and the page numbering format for an index in the Define Index dialog box.

To Generate the Index

After you've marked all the index entries or completed the concordance file, and also defined the index, follow these steps to generate it:

1.   From the **T**ools menu, choose **G**enerate (Alt-F5,4).

2.   Choose OK or press ↵.

Remember to use Generate again after editing your document and before printing it.

● **NOTES**   You can have more than one listing in the index for the same word or phrase. Simply select the text, mark the entry as usual, and repeat the process but enter a different heading and subheading.

To delete an index entry, display the Reveal Codes window and delete the index code.

● **SEE ALSO**   Copy/Copy and Paste, Page Numbering, Reveal Codes, Select, Sort and Select, Styles

INITIAL CODES

If you create most documents using the same format and layout, you can save some time by defining the Initial Codes Setup. You can insert the commands and options you usually select into the Initial Codes Setup. Each time you begin a new document, Word-Perfect will apply those commands and options.

You can define the Initial Codes for all documents by using the Initial Codes Setup feature or you can define them for your current document by using the Document Initial Codes feature.

To Change the Default Initial Codes

1.   From the Layout menu, choose Document (Shift-F8,4).

2.   Choose Initial Codes Setup (2).

3.   To insert codes in this window, choose the commands from the menus and use the keystrokes as you normally do. The menu bar is still visible and active at the top of the screen.

4.   When you are finished, press F7 to close the window.

5.   Choose OK or press ↵ to close the dialog box. If you used (Shift-F8, 4) press ↵ again to choose Close.

To Change Initial Codes for the Current Document

1.   From the Layout menu, choose Document (Shift-F8,4.

2.   Choose Document Initial Codes (1).

3.   To insert codes in this window, choose the commands from the menus and use the keystrokes as you normally do. The menu bar is still visible and active at the top of the screen.

4.   When you are finished, press F7 to close the window.

5.   Choose OK or press ↵ to close the dialog box. If you used (Shift-F8,4) press ↵ again to choose Close.

When you insert a code in the Document Initial Codes window, it overrides any conflicting code in the Initial Codes Setup window. For example, if you have page numbering set to print at the bottom of each page in the Initial Codes Setup window and you select No Page Numbering in the Document Initial Codes window, page numbers will not be printed in the current document.

To Modify Initial Codes

1.   From the Layout menu, choose Document (Shift-F8,4).

2.   Choose either Initial Codes Setup (2) or Document Initial Codes (1).

3.   Choose additional commands to insert as needed.

4.   To delete a code, highlight it and press Delete.

5.   When you are finished, press F7 to close the window.

6.   Choose OK or press ↵ to close the dialog box. If you used (Shift-F8,4) press ↵ again to choose Close.

When you change the Initial Codes Setup, the changes are applied to new documents only.

• **NOTES**   Initial Codes do not appear at the top of your document. You cannot see them initially when you display the Reveal Codes window. However, when you highlight the [Initial Codes] code, the additional codes are displayed.

Any formatting or layout changes you make within a document are always applied and override both Initial Codes Setup and Document Initial Codes. If you retrieve an existing document (Document A) into another document (Document B), it does not keep its initial codes, but instead the codes in effect for Document B are applied to Document A.

All WordPerfect formatting features can be inserted as Initial Codes, except the Envelope feature. You can define initial codes from anywhere in a document; the entire document is always affected.

• **SEE ALSO**   Codes, Reveal Codes

INSERT MODE

WordPerfect is normally in Insert mode, which means that all text, spacing, line and page breaks, and most codes are inserted at the location of the cursor. Any text, spacing, or codes to the right of the cursor are moved to accommodate the insertion.

When WordPerfect is in Insert mode, the left part of the status line shows whatever you've selected in the Screen Setup dialog box. When WordPerfect is not in Insert mode, it is in Typeover mode and the word *Typeover* appears there instead.

To Insert Text or Space

Use the following methods to insert text or spacing:

• To insert text, position the cursor where you want to insert it and type the text.

- To insert spaces, position the cursor where you want to insert them and press the spacebar.

- To insert lines, position the cursor where you want to insert them and press ↵ as many times as needed to add each new line.

You can position the cursor with the WordPerfect cursor movement keys or by clicking the mouse where you want the cursor to be.

● **SEE ALSO**   Typeover Mode, and inside the front cover for Cursor Movement Keys and Mouse Shortcuts

JUSTIFICATION

The Justification setting determines whether the document will have even left or right margins or be centered between the margins.

To Set the Justification

1. Position the cursor in the paragraph where you want the justification change to begin, or at the beginning of the document to change the justification for the entire document.

2. From the Layout menu, choose Justification.

3. Choose the type of justification you want.

Left	Text is aligned on the left margin only; the right margin is uneven.
Center	Text is centered between the left and right margins.
Right	Text is aligned on the right margin only; the left margin is uneven.
Full	Text is aligned on both the left and right margins. Spacing is adjusted between words to make the lines even.

Full, **A**ll Lines   Text is aligned on both the left and right
                        margins and the letters are evenly spaced
                        between the margins. Use this option to
                        justify titles and headings.

To Change the Justification for Selected Text

1. Select (block) the text to be justified.

2. From the **L**ayout menu, choose **J**ustification.

3. Choose the type of justification you want.

You can quickly change the justification by choosing Left, Center,
Right or Full from the Justification button in the middle of the ribbon. Click and hold the mouse over the button and select a different
setting. The Full and All Lines options are not available on the ribbon.

To Change the Justification for a Line

1. Position the cursor in the line.

2. From the **L**ayout menu, choose **L**ine (Shift-F8,1).

3. Select **J**ustification (2).

4. Select the type of justification you want—**L**eft, **C**enter,
       Right, **F**ull, or **A**ll lines—and press ↵.

5. Press ↵ to select OK, and press ↵ again to select Close if
       you used (Shift-F8,1).

● **NOTES**   If Auto Code Placement is not turned on, you'll need
to place the cursor at the top of the paragraph to be justified. Tables
within a document are not affected by the justification setting.

● **SEE ALSO**   Auto Code Placement, Center Text, Margins, Ribbon, Select, Tables

LANGUAGE

You can use the conventions of another language by selecting that language and applying it to either selected text, the current document, or all documents. Commands that are affected include Date, Hyphenation, Speller, and Thesaurus.

To Select a Different Language

To change the language for selected text:

1. Select (block) the text or position the cursor where you want the change to begin.

2. From the Layout menu, choose Other (Shift-F8,7).

3. Choose Language (7).

4. Either select a language from the list box or select Other Language Code and type a two-letter language code in the text box. Then choose OK or press ↵.

5. Choose OK or press ↵. If you used (Shift-F8,7) you have to press ↵ again to chose Close.

If you want all text, a "Continued..." message in the footnote, and the document summary to use another language's conventions, you have to change the language for the entire document:

1. From the Layout menu, choose Document (Shift-F8,4).

2. Choose Document Initial Codes (1).

3. Follow the preceding steps 2 through 5.

4. When you are finished, press F7 to close the window.

5. Choose OK or press ↵ to close the dialog box.

To select a language that will be applied to all new documents:

1. From the File menu, choose Setup (Shift-F1).

2. Choose Environment (3).

3. Choose Language (L).

4. Select a language from the list box and choose OK or press ↵.

5. Choose OK or press ↵. If you used Shift-F1, you need to press ↵ again to select Close.

● **NOTES**   WordPerfect uses the conventions of the language you select but does not support features such as Hyphenation, Speller, and Thesaurus unless you purchase and install an additional language module that contains the necessary information for that language.

● **SEE ALSO**   Date and Time, Hyphenation, Speller, Thesaurus

LINE DRAW

Line Draw lets you draw a line or box in your document by using the cursor keys. (You cannot draw a line with the mouse.) You can draw with a single or double line, most characters on the keyboard, or any of WordPerfect's special characters.

To Draw a Line in a Document

1. Position the cursor where you want to start drawing the line.

2. From the Graphics menu, choose Line Draw (Ctrl-F3,5).

3. From here you can:

● Select a character (1, 2, or 3) from the options at the bottom of the screen.

● Choose Change (4) to open the Change Line Draw Character dialog box and select another character (1 through 8).

● Use any other character by choosing Change (4), selecting User-defined (9), and typing the character. If you want to use a character from WordPerfect's special character set, press Ctrl-2 after selecting User-defined, enter the number of the character set, type a comma (,), enter the character number, and press ↵ (the numbers you press won't show on the screen). For example, to draw a line or box with stars (not asterisks), select User-defined (9), press Ctrl-2, press 6 (the number of the character set), type a comma, enter 184 (the character number), and press ↵. A star will be displayed next to the number 3 at the bottom of the screen.

4.   Use the keys in Table 7 to draw in any direction.

5.   Choose Close or press F7 when you are done.

Table 7 summarizes WordPerfect's line-drawing keys. You can change the character at any time while you are drawing by selecting 1, 2, 3, or 4.

Table 7: Line Draw Keystrokes

Keys	Extends the Line
↑, ↓, →, ←	One character at a time in the direction of the arrow.
Home, Home-↑	To the top margin.
Home, Home-↓	To the bottom margin.
Home, Home-→	To the right margin.
Home, Home-←	To the left margin.

To Delete a Line

- To delete a line while you are drawing, choose Erase (5) and use the arrow keys.

- To delete part of a line or box from the document window, position the cursor where you want to begin deleting and press Delete to delete to the right or Backspace to delete to the left.

- To delete an entire line or box, select (block) it and press Delete.

● **NOTES** WordPerfect automatically turns on Typeover mode when you choose Line Draw and fills boxes with spaces and hard returns. If you want to add text inside a box once you are back in the document window, make sure you are in Typeover mode.

To create a line or box and control the thickness or shading, use the Graphics Lines or Graphics Boxes commands. Or, add a Border and select a predefined style.

Line Draw only works with nonproportional (fixed-width) fonts.

● **SEE ALSO** Borders, Graphics Boxes, Graphics Lines, Typeover Mode, WP Characters

LINE HEIGHT

You can specify the distance between the baseline (bottom) of each line, and therefore, the space allotted to each line of text, by setting the line height.

To Set the Line Height

1. Position the cursor where you want to begin the change.
2. From the Layout menu, choose Line (Shift-F8,1).
3. Select Line Height (8), select Fixed (2), type the number in the text box, and press ↵

The Auto Line Height setting causes WordPerfect to automatically adjust the height to accommodate the largest font on the line. The Fixed setting causes WordPerfect to use the height you specify, regardless of the font size.

4. Choose OK or press ↵. If you used (Shift-F8,1) you must press ↵ again to select Close.

● **SEE ALSO** Line Spacing

LINE NUMBERING

You can number the lines in a document and also specify where and how you want the numbers displayed. Headers, footers, footnotes, and endnotes are not counted or numbered.

To Add Line Numbers to a Document

1. Position the cursor where you want to begin the numbering.

2. From the Layout menu, choose Line (Shift-F8,1).

3. Select Line Numbering (4) and check Line Numbering On (1). You can change any of the options in the dialog box (see "Line Numbering Options").

4. Choose OK or press ↵ to close the Line Numbering Format dialog box.

5. Choose OK or press ↵. If you used (Shift-F8,1) you must press ↵ again to select Close.

You can change the line numbering format anywhere in your document by following the previous steps and making changes in the Line Numbering Format dialog box.

To Discontinue Line Numbers

1. Position the cursor where you want to end the numbering.

2. From the Layout menu, choose Line (Shift-F8,1).

3. Select Line Numbering (4) and remove the check from Line Numbering On (1).

4. Choose OK or press ↵ twice, and then press ↵ again to select Close.

Line Numbering Options

The following options in the Line Numbering Format dialog box let you customize the line numbering. The Sample Numbering box on the right in the dialog box shows the result of your selections.

Starting Line Number (2)	Enter the number at which WordPerfect should begin counting.
First Line Number Printed (3)	Enter the number at which WordPerfect should begin printing line numbers.
Numbering **I**nterval (4)	Specify how often WordPerfect should print line numbers. For example, to print line numbers on every fifth line, enter 5.
Numbering **M**ethod (5)	Select the type of characters WordPerfect should print as line numbers. The options are for numbers, upper- and lowercase letters, and upper- and lowercase roman numerals.
Position of Number (6)	Specify where WordPerfect should print line numbers. Select either From Left Edge of Page or Relative to Margin and enter the distance in the text box.
Restart Numbering on Each Page (7)	Check this option to have WordPerfect begin recounting at the top of each page, using the Starting Line Number.
Count Blank Lines (8)	Check this option to make WordPerfect count blank lines; leave it unchecked to make WordPerfect skip blank lines.
Number all **N**ewspaper Columns (9)	If your documented is formatted in newspaper-style columns, check this option to have WordPerfect count the lines in each column, instead of the lines on the page.
Font/**A**ttributes/ Color (A)	Opens the Font dialog box where you change the attributes of the font used for numbering. WordPerfect uses the initial base font if you do not make any changes.

WP DOS

● **NOTES**   You cannot view line numbering in Text mode; switch to Page mode (Ctrl-F3,4) or Graphics mode (Ctrl-F3,3) to display it. However, line numbering will still print correctly in your document if you are running in Text mode.

● **SEE ALSO**   Columns, Font, Font Attributes

LINE SPACING

You can use the Line Spacing option to increase or decrease the space between lines of text. Normally, WordPerfect uses single spacing.

To Set the Line Spacing

1. Position the cursor where you want to begin the change.

2. From the Layout menu, choose Line (Shift-F8,1).

3. Select Line Spacing (3) and change the number in the text box. For double-spacing, enter **2.0** and press ↵.

4. Choose OK or press ↵. Press ↵ again to select Close if you used (Shift-F8,1).

● **NOTES**   The Line Height is multiplied by the Line Spacing to determine the space WordPerfect applies from baseline to baseline.

● **SEE ALSO**   Line Height

LISTS

You can have WordPerfect automatically generate a list of certain items within your document. For example, you could generate a list

of captions, figures, tables, or illustrations. More than one list can be defined and generated within a document.

To Mark List Entries

1. Select (block) the text you want to mark as an entry in the list.

2. From the Tools menu, choose List, and then Mark (Alt-F5,2)

3. Type the name of the list you are creating and press ↵.

If you typed the name of the list when you marked a previous entry, you can choose Lists and select one from the list box instead of retyping it each time.

Repeat the steps to mark each list entry. When you are finished, define the list.

To Define the List Location

You can define the location for the list and the numbering format.

1. Position the cursor at the end of the document or at an alternate location where you want the list to appear.

2. To begin the list on a new page, enter a page break by pressing Ctrl-↵. You may also want to enter a title for the list and add another blank line after it.

3. From the Tools menu, choose List, and then choose Define (Alt-F5,2,2).

4. In the list box, highlight the name of the list you want to define and select Edit (3).

5. Select a Numbering Mode from the options.

None (3)   No page numbers are included with the list entries.

Follows Entry (4)   The page numbers are placed after the entries.

(#) Follows Entry (5)	The page numbers are placed in parentheses after the entries.
# Flush Right (6)	The page numbers are right-justified.
...# Flush Right (7)	The page numbers are right-justified and preceded by a dot leader. (This is the default.)

6. Choose OK or press ↵.

7. Choose Select (1) to define the list.

You can also modify the list style and the page numbering format for a list in the Define List dialog box.

To Generate the List

After you've marked all the list entries and also defined the list, you can generate it.

1. From the Tools menu, choose Generate (Alt-F5,4).

2. Choose OK or press ↵.

Remember to use Generate again after editing your document and before printing it.

To List Captions

WordPerfect can also automatically generate a list of captions associated with the graphic boxes you created in your document.

1. Position the cursor at the end of the document or at an alternate location where you want the list to appear.

2. To begin the list on a new page, enter a page break by pressing Ctrl-↵.

3. From the Tools menu, choose List, and then choose Define (Alt-F5,2,2).

4. Select Create (2).

5. Type a name for the list in the Name text box and press ↵.

6. Select a Numbering Mode from the options.

7. Choose Include Graphics (9).

8. Highlight the type of graphics box in the list box and press ↵. Then choose Select. For example, if you want to generate a list of all the captions you've entered for the figures you created, select Figure Box from the list.

9. Choose OK or press ↵.

10. Choose Close in the Define List box. If you used (Alt-F5,2,2) in step 3, select OK in the Mark dialog box.

After you create the list, follow the previous steps to generate it.

● **SEE ALSO**   Graphics Boxes, Page Numbering, Styles

MACROS

WordPerfect's macro recorder lets you record the actions you perform repeatedly and save them in a file so you can play them back at any time. You can record keystrokes such as text you type on a regular basis, keystrokes to select several commands in sequence, and menu and dialog box selections. You can also record mouse actions with the exception of scrolling the document and positioning the cursor.

To Record a Macro

1. From the Tools menu, choose Macro.

2. Choose Record.

Ctrl-F10 starts macro recording in one step.

3. In the Macro text box, type the name of the macro. WordPerfect automatically assigns the file extension .WPM. Or, if you want to be able to play back the macro by pressing an Alt-key combination, press those keys now to assign

them to the macro. They will be displayed in the Macro text box.

4. Choose OK or press ↵ to begin recording. The document window is opened and "Recording Macro" is displayed in the lower-left corner of the screen.

5. Record the macro by typing text, entering keystrokes, and choosing menus, commands and options you want to include.

6. When you are finished, choose **M**acro from the **T**ools menu and choose **S**top (Ctrl-F10). WordPerfect compiles the macro and returns you to the document window.

WordPerfect records everything, including your mistakes, while you are recording. You may want to edit the macro when you are finished recording, or cancel the macro and start over if you inadvertently include some actions you did not intend to record.

To Pause a Macro

If you find you need to perform some actions that you don't want recorded as part of the macro, you can pause the macro recording temporarily.

1. From the **T**ools menu, choose **M**acro, and then choose **C**ontrol (Ctrl-Page Up).

2. In the Macro Control dialog box, check Macro Record **P**aused (2).

3. Choose OK or press ↵.

To later resume macro recording:

1. From the **T**ools menu, choose **M**acro, and then choose **C**ontrol (Ctrl-Page Up).

2. In the Macro Control dialog box, remove the check from Macro Record **P**aused (2).

3. Choose OK or press ↵.

To Assign a Macro to a Button

Once you record a macro you can assign it to the button bar. The new button will show the name of the macro and a picture of a tape cassette as well if you have your button bar set up to show pictures.

1. From the View menu, choose Button Bar Setup.

2. Choose Edit.

3. Select Add Macro (3) to add a macro, highlight the macro in the list box and choose Select.

A new button is added to the end of the button bar. Use Move Button (6) to move it to a new location, if you wish.

4. When you are finished modifying the button bar, choose OK or press Tab and then ⏎.

To Select and Run a Macro

You can play macros you've recorded or written, macros an associate has written for you, and any of the macros shipped with WordPerfect.

There are two quick ways to run macros:

- If you've assigned the macro to an Alt-key combination, you can run the macro by pressing those keys.

- If you've assigned the macro to a button on your button bar, you can run the macro by clicking the button.

Otherwise, follow these steps to run a macro:

1. From the Tools menu, choose Macro Play (Alt-F10).

2. In the Macro text box, type the name of the macro or select it from the drop-down list.

You can use the File List (F5) button to display all the files in the WP60\MACROS directory and then select any file with a .WPM extension from the list. The macro files shipped with WordPerfect, as well as those written and recorded in WordPerfect, are all given the .WPM extension.

WordPerfect compiles the macro before it is run, so you may briefly see the message "Compiling Macro" before the macro is executed. Whether you see this message depends on the complexity of the macro and the computer you are working on.

To Edit an Existing Macro

You can edit macros you've recorded, written, or converted from WordPerfect 5.1, as well as those shipped with WordPerfect. Macros are stored by WordPerfect as document files.

1. From the Tools menu, choose **M**acro **R**ecord (Ctrl-F10).

2. In the Macro text box, type the name of the macro to edit, or select it from the drop-down list box. You can also use File List (F5) or QuickList (F6).

3. Check **E**dit Macro (2) and choose OK or choose **E**dit if you used File List or QuickList. The document window is opened with the contents of the macro and "Edit Macro" is displayed in the lower-left corner of the screen.

4. Edit the macro by typing or deleting text. Most editing features are available from this window.

5. If you want to record additional commands, press Shift-F3 to switch to recording mode and then record. When you are finished, press Shift-F3 to switch back to editing mode.

6. When you are finished editing, choose **M**acro from the Tools menu and then choose **S**top (Ctrl-F10). WordPerfect compiles the macro and returns you to the document window with the macro script displayed. Use Save (Ctrl-F12) when you have finished editing.

To Assign a Macro to a Hotkey

If you create a macro and later want to assign it to an Alt-letter hotkey combination, you can do this by using the Keyboard Layout feature under Setup in the File menu.

1. From the File menu, choose Se**t**up (Shift-F1).

2. Choose **K**eyboard Layout (4).

3. In the list box, highlight the name of the keyboard you want to assign the macro to. The one you are currently using has an asterisk. Then choose Edit (3). You cannot edit the Original keyboard. See the "Setup" entry if you want to create a new keyboard.

4. Choose Create (1).

5. Press the keystrokes to which you want to assign the macro in order to enter them in the Key text box. For example, if you want to assign an existing macro to the keystrokes Alt-D, press Alt-D at the keyboard.

6. Choose Macro (5), select Retrieve Macro (2), and enter the name of the macro in the list box.

7. Choose OK or press Tab and then ↵ until all the dialog boxes are closed.

● **NOTES** WordPerfect also includes a very powerful macro language that you can use to write macros instead of recording them. The macro language is not described in this book, but is described in the WordPerfect documentation and in *Mastering WordPerfect 6 for DOS*, also published by Sybex.

A macro conversion utility that lets you covert WordPerfect 5.1 macros is included with WordPerfect 6.0.

● **SEE ALSO** Button Bar, Macro Conversion, Save, Setup

MACRO CONVERSION

If you try to select and run a macro created with WordPerfect 5.1, you will see an error message because 5.1 macros cannot be run with Version 6.0. However, WordPerfect provides a macro conversion program so that you can convert macros you recorded or wrote with WordPerfect 5.1 to macros that can be used with Word-Perfect 6.0. Since there have been some keystroke and command changes, you may still need to edit some of your macros after you convert them.

To Convert Existing Macros

The macro conversion program must be run from the DOS prompt. You can either exit WordPerfect or use the Go to Shell command to shell out to the DOS prompt temporarily.

1. At the DOS prompt, type **cd WP60** and press ↵.

2. At the WP60 prompt, type **mcv**. You'll see the prompt "Input file or pattern."

3. Type the path and name of the file you want to convert. For example, to convert a macro file in the WP51 directory on C:, type C:\WP51*filename*.wpm. To convert all the macro files in the WP51 directory on C:, type C:\WP51\ *.wpm. Then press ↵.

You'll see the prompt "Output file or path."

4. Type the path and/or name of the file you want to convert. For example, to convert a macro file in the WP51 directory to a macro file in the WP60 directory on C:, type C:\WP60. WordPerfect will create a file of the same name at the new location. Press ↵ after you enter the destination.

WordPerfect converts each file and then lists it on the screen. You can convert additional macros by following steps 2 through 4.

Macro Conversion Options

The following options are available when you run the macro conversion utility.

/b (block)	Assumes that block is on at the start of each macro.
/h (help)	Displays a list of all macro conversion options.

/l (logfile)	Creates a file that saves all the messages displayed on the screen during conversion.
/o (override)	Replaces existing files with converted files of the same name without prompting you for confirmation.
/q (quotes)	Deletes the outside quote marks from strings in expressions.
/s (short)	Uses short token names.

To use one or more options, type mcv [option] [source] [destination] and press ↵, or simply type mcv and press ↵ to have Word-Perfect prompt you for the source and destination.

● **NOTES**   When entering the input (source) file for the conversion, you can use the wildcard characters * and ?. However, if you do, the output (destination) must be a volume or directory, not an individual file name. If you do not use the /o option, you'll be prompted before WordPerfect copies over any existing files of the same name at the destination.

● **SEE ALSO**   Exit Document/Exit, Go to Shell, Macros

MARGINS

You can change the left, right, top, and bottom margins of a document at any time. You can also reset the left and right margins for one or more paragraphs, automatically indent first lines, and specify additional spacing between paragraphs.

To Set Document Margins

1. Position the cursor where you want to change the margins.

2. From the Layout menu, choose Margins (Shift-F8,2).

3. In the Document Margins area, select the Left (1), Right (2), Top (3), or Bottom (4) margin that you want to change and enter the new margin setting in the text box. Repeat the step for each margin you want to change.

4. Choose OK or press ↵. If you used (Shift-F8,2), press ↵ again to select Close.

The default document margins are 1 inch.

To Adjust Paragraph Margins

1. Select (block) the paragraphs to be affected or position the cursor where you want to begin the change.

2. From the Layout menu, choose Margins (Shift-F8,2).

3. Select the Paragraph Margins area, select the margin you want to change (5–8), and enter the new margin setting in the text box.

Left Margin Adjustment (5)	Enter a positive number to indent the paragraph; enter a negative number to release the margin and "outdent" the paragraph to the left.
Right Margin Adjustment (6)	Enter a positive number to indent the paragraph from the right; enter a negative number to release the margin and outdent the paragraph to the right.
First Line Indent (7)	Enter a number to automatically indent the first line of every paragraph by that amount.

| Paragraph Spacing (8) | Enter the number of lines to insert between paragraphs for additional spacing each time you enter a hard return. |

4. Choose OK or press ↵. If you used (Shift-F8,2), press ↵ to select Close.

To change the margin for one paragraph at a time, you can also use Indent.

● **NOTES**   To reset the margin back to normal, display the Reveal Codes window and delete the margin code. To change the margins for all documents, use Initial Codes Setup. To adjust the space at the margin in order to leave a binding edge, use Binding Offset.

● **SEE ALSO**   Binding Offset, Indent, Initial Codes, Line Spacing, Reveal Codes

MASTER DOCUMENT

A master document lets you control other WordPerfect documents and organize them into one large, cohesive document. You can use a master document to create a report or book from several sections or chapters (subdocuments). You can also make an existing document the master document.

To Create a Master Document

You can create a new document and use it as a master document, or you can make the first document the master document. The master document contains the links to the subdocuments.

1. From the File menu, choose New to create a new document, or choose Open (Shift-F10) and open the document you'll use.

2. Position the cursor where you want to link to the first sub-document.

3. From the File menu, choose Master Document (Alt-F5,3).

4. Choose Subdocument (3).

5. Enter the name of the document in the Filename text box. If the file is not saved in the same directory as the master document, enter the full path and file name. For example, you could enter C:\WP60\BOOK\CHAPTER1.WP.

6. Choose OK or press ↵.

7. Repeat steps 3 through 6 to insert additional links to each file you want to include as a subdocument.

If you are working in Text mode, the name of each subdocument is shown in the document window as a comment. In Graphics and Page mode, you'll have to look in the Reveal Codes window to see the name of each subdocument.

Master documents are saved like other WordPerfect documents, but you can also condense a master document when you save it.

Printing and Viewing the Subdocuments

When you want to print the entire document or view all the sub-documents in sequence, expand the master document. When you expand the master document, WordPerfect retrieves all the sub-documents and inserts them at the location of the links.

1. From the File menu, choose Master Document (Alt-F5,3).

2. Choose Expand (1). All the subdocuments are shown in the Subdocuments list box.

3. If there are subdocuments you do not want to expand, highlight them and press the asterisk (*) key or spacebar to unmark them.

4. Choose OK and then choose Yes to expand the marked subdocuments.

If a subdocument can't be found in the current directory, Word-Perfect prompts you to enter its file name. You can enter the name or skip the file when you see this dialog box.

To Condense a Master Document

When you condense the master document, WordPerfect deletes the contents of the subdocuments, but saves the links.

1. From the File menu, choose Master Document (Alt-F5,3).

2. Choose Condense (2). All the subdocuments are shown in the Subdocuments list box.

3. If there are subdocuments you do not want to condense, highlight them and press the asterisk key or spacebar to unmark them.

4. To save any documents you've made edits to, highlight each and select Save Subdoc (1) or move the cursor anywhere in the list box and select Save All (2).

5. Choose OK and then choose Yes to condense the marked subdocuments.

Generating Indexes, Lists, Footnotes, Etc.

It's best to mark all text for tables of contents, indexes, footnotes and endnotes, tables of authorities, lists, and cross-references in the subdocuments. When you define where these items are to be located, you can choose either the master document or subdocuments. The master document does not have to be expanded before you choose Generate. WordPerfect will expand it, generate the index or list, and then condense the master document, allowing you to save any modified subdocuments.

● **NOTES**   To delete a subdocument, display the Reveal Codes window and delete the subdocument code.

Formatting changes made in either a master document or subdocument are in effect until a new setting appears. Styles in subdocuments do not affect styles in the master document.

When you expand a master document prior to printing, the subdocuments are formatted for the selected printer. If this printer is different from the one selected when they were edited, fonts and other formatting may change.

● **SEE ALSO**   Comments, Footnotes and Endnotes, Index, Lists, Print, Reveal Codes, Save/Save As, Table of Authorities, Table of Contents

MATH

WordPerfect's Math feature lets you perform basic mathematical calculations within a document. Math organizes data within columns, not within a spreadsheet as the Table feature does.

To Turn Math On and Off

Before you turn math on, you may want to use the Tab Set command to adjust (widen) the columns; the columns are aligned based on the tab stops.

To turn Math on:

1. Position the cursor where you want to begin inserting the data.

2. From the Tools menu, choose Math, and then choose On. You can also press Alt-F7,3,1 ↵.

3. Enter your data (see the next section for how to do this).

You can turn the Math feature on and off as needed within a document in order to include mathematical information in several locations.

When you finish entering data:

1. Position the cursor where you want to stop calculating.

2. From the Tools menu, choose Math, and then choose Off. You can also press Alt-F7,3,1 ↵.

To Enter Data

Once Math is turned on, you can enter the data in all but the first column, as follows:

1. Press Tab to position the cursor in the second column.

2. Type the number and press Tab to move to the next column to the right. Numbers are aligned on the decimal character.

The space between the margin and the first tab stop is not included when math calculations are performed, so always begin entering data after the first tab stop.

3. Repeat step 2 until you've entered all the numbers in the first row, and then press ↵.

4. Repeat steps 1 through 3 until you've entered all the numbers.

5. To calculate the subtotal or total at the bottom of each column, enter the appropriate function from Table 8 at that location. For example, to calculate the subtotal of the numbers entered in the first column, enter a plus sign (+) at the bottom of the column. (See "Calculating Column Totals with Functions" for information.)

Table 8: Functions for Calculating Column Totals

Function Character	Result
+ (subtotal)	Adds the numbers in the above column.
= (total)	Adds the subtotals in the above column.
* (grand total)	Adds the totals in the above column.
t (extra subtotal)	Includes the number when subtotals are calculated.
T (extra total)	Includes the number when totals are calculated.
N (math negative)	Includes the number as a negative when subtotals or totals are calculated; N can be used with other functions.

To Label Rows and Columns

1. To include titles for your columns, position the cursor at the end of the line above where you turned Math on and press ⏎ to add a line. Press ↑ to move the cursor to the line you just added.

2. Type the column titles across this line, pressing Tab between each one.

3. To include labels for your rows, position the cursor at the left margin before the first tab stop.

4. Type the first row label and then press ↓ and ← to move to the beginning of the next line. You might need to press ← more than once. Type the next label below and press ↓ and ← until you've entered all the labels.

To Calculate Totals

To calculate or recalculate totals at any time:

- If there is only one Math section in the document, from the Tools menu choose Math and then choose Calculate (Alt-F7,3,3,).

- If there is more than one Math section in the document, position the cursor in each Math section ("Math" is shown in the status bar) and choose Calculate.

Calculating Column Totals with Functions

Functions tell WordPerfect how to calculate column totals. When you enter a function, the total is not shown until you choose Calculate. After you calculate, the function symbol is still shown on the screen next to the total, but not printed.

In order to use the t, T, or N functions, you must insert them next to the numbers that you want to affect.

Functions must be entered in the following order, from top to bottom, for WordPerfect to correctly calculate them:

- + (subtotal), t (extra subtotal)

- = (total), T (extra total)

- * (grand total)

● **NOTES** If you need to perform more advanced calculations, you can define the columns in such a way that the Math feature can perform these tasks, or you can use the Spreadsheet or Tables feature instead. Refer to your WordPerfect documentation for more information on defining columns; spreadsheets and tables are discussed elsewhere in this book.

You can have up to 24 columns across, and use either absolute or relative tab stops to separate the columns. All math columns (beginning after the first tab stop) are predefined as numeric. You can include positive and negative numbers in the column to calculate a subtotal, total, or grand total and display it below.

The Decimal Alignment setting also affects the way totals are displayed.

● **SEE ALSO** Decimal Alignment, Spreadsheet, Tables, Tabs

MENUS

You can easily choose commands and features from WordPerfect's pull-down menus. Figure 8 shows the basic menu elements.

- An ellipsis (...) after a command means that when you choose it a dialog box is displayed.

- A triangle after a command means that when you choose it, another menu, sometimes called a cascading menu, is displayed.

- Keys displayed to the right of the command provide an alternate way to select the command.

- Items with a check (in Graphics mode) or an asterisk (in Text mode) are currently active.

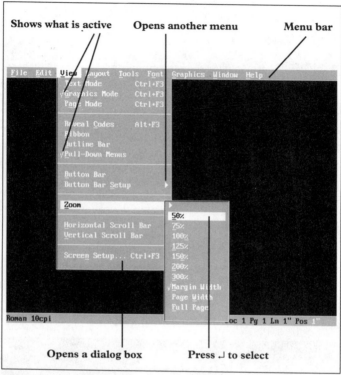

Figure 8: Menu elements

To Turn the Menu Bar Display On and Off

The menu bar shows the title of each menu. To display it, from the View menu choose Pull-Down Menus. Pull-Down Menus is checked or starred (depending on the current viewing mode) on the View menu when the menu bar is active. Choose Pull-Down Menus again at any time to turn off the display.

You can use pull-down menus whether or not the menu bar is displayed.

To Choose Items with Keys

If pull-down menus are not displayed, you can press Alt-= to display them temporarily in order to choose a command from them.

To move around the menus and select items with keys, use any of these methods:

1. Press Alt-= to position the cursor in the menu bar.

2. Press → or ← to move the cursor to the menu you want to open.

3. Press ↓ to open the menu and move the cursor to the item you want to choose.

4. Press ↵ to activate the command. If another menu is opened, press ↓ to move the cursor to the item you want to choose and press ↵.

Or, use this method:

1. Press Alt-= to position the cursor in the menu bar.

2. Press the highlighted (bolded or underlined) letter in the menu name to select and open the menu.

3. Press the highlighted letter in the command name or press the shortcuts keys shown on the menu to choose the command. If another menu is opened, press the highlighted letter in the command or option you want to select.

To Choose Items with the Mouse

- If pull-down menus are not displayed, click the right mouse button to display them temporarily in order to choose a command.

- To move around the menus and select commands with the mouse, simply click the menu title and then the command name on the menu.

● **NOTES**   You can activate the menus with the Alt key alone, instead of Alt-=, by checking the Alt key activities menus (2) option in the Screen Setup dialog box. You can also activate commands in one step by pressing Alt and the highlighted letter. However, if you have written or recorded Alt-key macros that can be activated by Alt-hotkey combinations, the macros are activated instead.

You can change menu colors by using the File Setup Display feature.

● **SEE ALSO**   Dialog Boxes, Macros, Screen Setup, Setup

MERGE

The Merge feature lets you combine the information in two separate files to create a new document. The most common use of merge is in the production of personalized form letters. However, merge can also help you quickly create contracts, memos, mailing labels, envelopes, or boilerplate documents.

To use merge, you'll create a data file and a form file. The data file shown in Figure 9 contains the information that changes in each document. The form file, shown in Figure 10, contains information that remains constant. These files can be created in any order. The data file and form file are merged to produce the final document, as shown in Figure 11.

Data Files

Data files are organized into records. A record is a group of related fields. For example, in a data file composed of addresses, each listing of a name and address would comprise one record. Within each record, the name, street address, city, state, and zip code may each be a separate field. Each record can contain as much information (as many fields) as is needed. Each data file can contain as many records as needed.

To Create a Data File

Follow these steps to create a data file similar to the one shown.

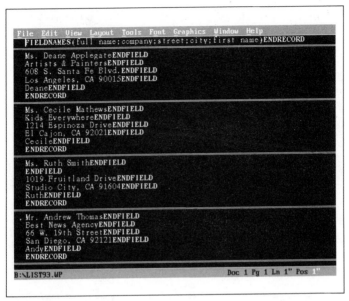

File Edit View Layout Tools Font Graphics Window Help
FIELDNAMES(full name;company;street;city;first name)ENDRECORD

Ms. Deane Applegate**ENDFIELD**
Artists & Painters**ENDFIELD**
608 S. Santa Fe Blvd.**ENDFIELD**
Los Angeles, CA 90015**ENDFIELD**
Deane**ENDFIELD**
ENDRECORD

Ms. Cecile Mathews**ENDFIELD**
Kids Everywhere**ENDFIELD**
1214 Espinoza Drive**ENDFIELD**
El Cajon, CA 92021**ENDFIELD**
Cecile**ENDFIELD**
ENDRECORD

Ms. Ruth Smith**ENDFIELD**
ENDFIELD
1019.Fruitland Drive**ENDFIELD**
Studio City, CA 91604**ENDFIELD**
Ruth**ENDFIELD**
ENDRECORD

. Mr. Andrew Thomas**ENDFIELD**
Best News Agency**ENDFIELD**
66 W. 19th Street**ENDFIELD**
San Diego, CA 92121**ENDFIELD**
Andy**ENDFIELD**
ENDRECORD

B:\LIST93.WP   Doc 1 Pg 1 Ln 1" Pos 1"

Figure 9: A data file (name and address list)

1. Choose **New** from the **File** menu to open a new document.

2. Type the name of the first person in the list; do not insert a space after the name.

3. From the **Tools** menu, choose **Merge**, and choose **Define** (Shift-F9).

4. Select **Data** [Text] (2).

5. Select End **Field** (1). The ENDFIELD code appears at the end of the name and the cursor is positioned on the next line.

6. Type the next line. In a mailing list, this might be a company name or the first line of the address.

7. From the **Tools** menu, choose **Merge**, choose **Define** (Shift-F9), and then select End Field (1) or just press F9.

8. Repeat steps 6 and 7 until you have completed the information for the first name and address.

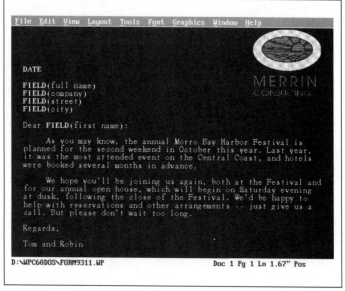

Figure 10: A form file (form letter)

9. From the Tools menu, choose Merge, choose Define (Shift-F9), and then select End Record (2). The ENDRECORD code appears on the next line and is followed by a page break.

10. Repeat steps 6 though 9 until you've added all the records (names and addresses) to your list.

11. From the File menu, choose Save (Ctrl-F12), enter a name for the file, and choose OK.

Do not leave extra spaces at the end of lines or between data fields. Make sure each record contains the same number of fields. If a field is not applicable, just leave it blank. For example, if you have a field for company names but one person on your list is self-employed and does not work for a company, leave the company field blank. Make sure the order in which you enter the information in the fields remains the same from record to record. More than one line of information can be designated as a field and this does not have to be

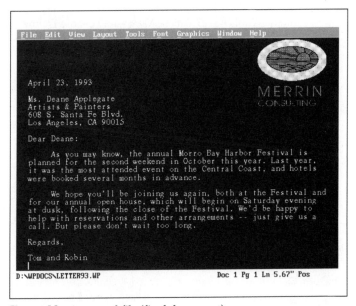

Figure 11: A merged file (final document)

the same in each record. For example, the address line (street, suite number, P.O. Box) might require one line in some cases and two lines in others. When you need two lines, just press ↵ after the first line and press F9 at the end of the second line to insert an ENDFIELD code. Also, the same information can be included in more than one field. For example, you could designate the whole name as a field in order to place it on the envelopes ("Mr. Bob Smith") and designate the first name as another field in order to create personalized, first name greetings ("Dear Bob") in your letters.

To Define Field Names

It's helpful to define field names in order to keep track of the fields in your data file. If you do not define the names, WordPerfect will assign a number to each field. You can define the fields before or after you enter the data in the data file.

1. From the Tools menu, choose Merge, and choose Define (Shift-F9).

2. Select Field Names (3).

3. Enter a descriptive name for the first field in the Field Name text box and press ↵.

4. Continue entering descriptive names for each field, and make sure you enter the names in the right order. Press ↵ after you enter each name.

5. Choose OK. The field names will be displayed at the top of the document window.

6. From the File menu, choose Save (Ctrl-F12) to save the document, and then choose Close from the File menu.

Form Files

The form file controls the merge operation. It contains the text, formatting, and graphics you want repeated in each merged record. Merge programming commands can also be inserted in the form file.

To Create a Form File

To create a form file, begin the document as usual and enter text until you reach the first place where you want to enter variable information. For example, in a form letter you'll want to enter the address from the mailing list. To insert variable information:

1. Position the cursor where you want to insert the first field.

2. From the Tools menu, choose Merge, and then choose Define (Shift-F9).

3. Select Form and choose OK.

4. Select Field (1), enter the Field Name (or number if you did not name the fields) in the text box, and choose OK. If necessary, select the List Field Names (F5) button to select the exact field names from your data file.

5. Continue entering text until you reach the next place in the document where you want to insert a variable, and then repeat steps 2 and 4.

6. Repeat this process until you finish the document.

7. To have the correct date inserted in the letter when it is merged, move the cursor where you want the date to appear, from the **T**ools menu select **M**erge, and then choose **D**efine (Shift-F9). Choose Merge Codes (Shift-F9), highlight DATE in the list box, and choose Select. The date format specified at the time of the merge is used.

8. From the File menu, choose **S**ave (Ctrl-F12) to save the document, and then choose **C**lose from the File menu.

When you create a form file, display the merge codes so that you can be sure you've entered the field information correctly. However, when you are finished creating the file, you can turn them off or display them as icons by selecting either option under Display of Merge Codes (4) in the Merge Codes dialog box.

To Merge Data and Form Files

When the data and form files are both complete, you can merge them to create the final file.

1. From the **T**ools menu, choose **M**erge, and then choose **R**un (Ctrl-F9,1).

2. Enter the name of the Form File (1) in the text box and press ⏎.

3. Enter the name of the Data File (2) in the text box and press ⏎.

4. Select an Output (3) option from the pop-up list.

Current Document	The merged file is output to and displayed in the current document window.
Unused Document	The merged file is output to and displayed in a new document window that WordPerfect opens.

| Printer | The merged file is printed to the selected printer; make sure the printer is ready to print. |
| File | The merged file is saved in a new file; enter a file name in the text box and press ⏎. |

5. Choose Data File Options (see "Data File Options" below) and specify options.

6. Choose Merge.

The files are merged. If you selected to view the output in a document window, review it on-screen and then either save the file or print it.

Data File Options

These data file options are available when performing a merge:

Repeat Merge for Each Data Record (4)	Enter the number of times you want the entire merge operation repeated, if you want it performed more than once.
Display of Merge Codes (5)	Select whether to show or hide codes or to display them as icons.
Blank Fields in Data Files (6)	Select whether to have WordPerfect remove or leave blank any lines that result when the corresponding data field is empty.
Page Break Between Merged Records (7)	Select to insert a page break after each record, so the next one always begins on a new page.
Generate an Envelope for Each Data Record (8)	Opens the Envelope dialog box where you can create an envelope form file to be included in the current form file.

| Data Record Selection Range (9) | Select the range of records you want to include in the merge. If you do not want to merge all the records in the data file, either mark the records, specify a range, or define conditions. |

To Define Field and Record End Characters

In addition to creating data files in WordPerfect, you can use files in ASCII-delimited format. Files created in a spreadsheet or database program that can be exported in ASCII-delimited text format can be used to create data files.

In order to merge these files, however, you must first identify the characters or codes that were used to define the fields and records. You can do this in Setup before you merge, with these steps:

1. From the File menu, choose Setup, and then choose Environment (Shift-F1,3).

2. Choose Delimited Text Options (D).

3. Select each applicable option and enter a character or press F5 and select a code from the pop-up box.

Field Delimiter (1)	Enter the character or code used to define the end of the field.
Record Delimiter (2)	Enter the character or code used to define the end of the record.
Field Encapsulate Character (3)	Enter the character or code used to enclose the field data.
Strip Characters (4)	Enter the character or code you want WordPerfect to remove from the data file.

4. When you are finished, choose OK.

You can also define the characters when you are ready to merge, with these steps:

1. From the Tools menu choose Merge, and then choose Run (Ctrl-F9,1).

2. Enter the name of the form file in the text box and press ↵.

3. Enter the name of the ASCII-delimited text file in the Data File text box.

4. DOS Delimited Text is highlighted in the File Format dialog box. Choose Select.

5. Select the applicable option and enter a character, or press F5 and select a code from the pop-up box.

6. Check Save Setup Options (5) if you want to reuse these settings, and then choose OK.

7. Choose Merge.

● **NOTES**   To cancel a merge at any time, press Esc or, if you've turned off the Esc/Cancel key, press Ctrl-Break. You can open or switch to another document window while a merge is in progress. If you include graphics in your form file, use the Image on Disk feature to speed up the merge operation. To get to this option, choose Graphics, Graphics Boxes, Edit, Contents, and Image on Disk.

WordPerfect also includes some very powerful merge programming commands. You can use them to add some features and flexibility during merge operations. The most common features are included in the Data File Options dialog box.

● **SEE ALSO**   Exit Document/Exit WP/Close, Date and Time, Envelope, Graphics Boxes, Save/Save As, Setup, Windows

The New command lets you start a new document and open it in a new window in one step.

To Create a New Document

To create a new, blank document:

- From the File menu, choose **New**.

New documents are opened using the Default Initial Codes. The cursor will be in the upper-left corner of the window.

When you start WordPerfect, a new, blank document window is opened automatically.

● **NOTES**   You can open an existing document by using Open or Retrieve.

● **SEE ALSO**   Open, Retrieve

The Open command lets you open an existing document in a new window in one step. Use it if you currently have one or more documents open and want to open another document in a new window without first closing any documents.

To Open an Existing Document

1. From the File menu, choose **O**pen (Shift-F10).
2. There are three ways to choose the file to open:
   - In the Filename (1) text box, enter the path and file name of the file you want to open. If the file is located in the default directory, you only need to enter the file name.
   - Select a file name from the drop-down list.

- Use File Manager (F5) or QuickList (F6) to select the file.

3. Choose OK or press ↵. Make sure the Method (2) selected is Open into New Document (1). You can press Shift-F10 to change the method.

If you change your mind and want to retrieve the document into the current document window, select Retrieve into Current Document (2) as the Method (2) in the Open Document dialog box before choosing OK.

To Convert a File

WordPerfect can open files created with many other applications so that you can edit them in WordPerfect 6.0. To convert a file:

1. From the File menu, choose Open (Shift-F10).

2. In the Filename (1) text box, enter the path and file name of the file you want to open. WordPerfect displays the File Format dialog box and selects the current format for the file.

3. If WordPerfect has correctly selected the file's format, choose Select. If it wasn't selected correctly, highlight the correct format in the list box and then choose Select.

The file is converted and opened in a new document window.

● **NOTES**   You can have up to nine documents in nine different document windows open at one time.

● **SEE ALSO**   File Manager, New, QuickList, Retrieve, Setup, Windows

OUTLINE

The Outline feature assigns numbers, letters, and bullets automatically to headings and paragraphs. You can use it to create an outline, number headings in a document, and number paragraphs.

To Create an Outline

1. Position the cursor where you want to begin the outline.

2. From the Tools menu, choose Outline (Ctrl-F5).

3. Choose Begin New Outline (1).

4. In the list box, highlight the outline style you want to use and choose Select (1).

5. Type the first outline text and press ↵.

6. Add additional entries with these techniques:

- To add another entry at the same level as the previous one, type the text and press ↵.
- To add another entry at a subordinate level from the previous one, press Tab to indent the line to the right an additional level, type the text, and press ↵.
- To add another entry at a higher level from the previous one, press Shift-Tab to move the line one level closer to the margin, type the text, and press ↵.

7. Repeat steps 5 and 6 until you complete the outline.

8. From the Tools menu, choose Outline (Ctrl-F5), and choose End Outline (5).

To Renumber an Outline

If you stop and then restart the outline in a document, first follow the steps to create an outline, and then follow these steps to renumber it:

1. Position the cursor where you want to begin renumbering.

2. From the Tools menu, choose Outline and then choose Outline Options (Ctrl-F5).

3. In the Set Paragraph Number (4) text box, enter the number you want to start at, using Arabic numbers separated

by commas, spaces, or periods. For example, to start at
III.D.5, enter 3,4,5, or 3 4 5, or 3.4.5.

4. Choose OK or press ⏎.

To Move, Copy, or Cut an Outline Family

An outline family is the text on the current line and the number, letter, or bullet to its left, as well as all subordinate entries below it,
including body text. To move, copy, or delete a family:

1. Position the cursor in the top line of the family you want
to move, copy, or delete.

2. From the Tools menu, choose Outline.

3. Choose Move Family, Copy Family, or Cut Family.

You can also press Ctrl-F5, select Move/Copy (M), and then select
Move Family (1), Copy Family (2), or Cut Family (3).

If you are moving or copying a family, move the cursor to the new
location and press ⏎.

You can paste the family into another outline by selecting Edit Paste
(Ctrl-V), or by selecting Tools Outline Paste (Ctrl-F5,M,4).

Moving around the Outline

Use the keys in Table 9 to move around the outline as you edit.

Table 9: Moving the Cursor in an Outline

Keys	Moves the Cursor to
Alt-↓	The next item at the same or higher level
Alt-↑	The previous item at the same or higher level
Alt-→	The next outline item
Alt-←	The previous outline item

- **NOTES**   Each outline entry is considered a paragraph because each entry ends with a hard return. The Outline feature also lets you number paragraphs.

You can also create and edit outline styles.

- **SEE ALSO**   Outline Bar, Paragraph Numbering, Styles

The Outline Bar provides access to many of the commands and options on the Outline menu and in the Outline dialog box. When the Outline Bar is active, the Outline menu is not available.

To Use the Outline Bar

- To display the Outline Bar, choose **O**utline Bar from the **V**iew menu, or press Ctrl-F5,7 to select the Display Outline Bar check box.

- To activate the Outline Bar, press Ctrl-O when the Outline Bar is displayed.

- To deactivate the Outline Bar, press Ctrl-O or F7.

Figure 12 shows the main elements of the Outline Bar. Refer to Table 10 to see what these options do.

- **SEE ALSO**   Outline, Styles

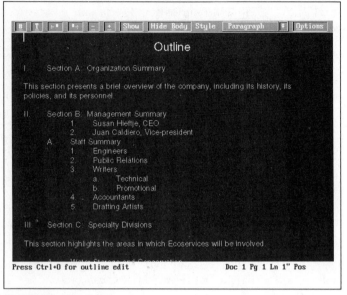

Figure 12: The Outline Bar

Table 10: Outline Bar Controls

Control	Purpose
#	Changes the current normal text to an outline item.
T	Changes the current outline item to normal text.
■←	Moves all items in the current family one level higher (to the left).
■→	Moves all items in the current family one level lower (to the right).
−	Hides the current family if it is a subordinate of a larger family.
+	Causes a hidden family to be displayed.

Table 10: Outline Bar Controls (continued)

Control	Purpose
Show	Shows the numbers of levels in the outline up to the level you specify.
Hide Body	Hides body text within the outline.
Show Body	Displays currently hidden body text within the outline.
Style	Lets you change the style of the outline.
Options	Opens the Outline dialog box where you can modify additional options.

OVERSTRIKE

You can create characters not available on your keyboard by printing two or more characters on top of each other. Use Overstrike to enter those characters.

To Create an Overstrike Character

1. Position the cursor where you want to create the overstrike character.

2. From the Layout menu, choose Character (Shift-F8,6).

3. Choose Create Overstrike (5).

4. If you want to change the attributes, choose Attributes (Ctrl-F8) and make the selection in the dialog box.

5. In the Overstrike Characters text box, type the characters you want printed as overstrike characters and press ↵. Do not include spaces.

6. Choose OK or press ↵.

You can see the overstrike character by switching to Page mode (Ctrl-F3,4) or Graphics mode (Ctrl-F3,3).

To Edit an Overstrike Character

1.   Position the cursor in front of the overstrike character.

2.   From the Layout menu, choose Character (Shift-F8,6).

3.   Choose Edit Overstrike (6).

4.   Add or delete the characters in the Overstrike Characters text box and press ↵.

5.   Choose OK or press ↵.

● **NOTES**   To delete an overstrike character, display the Reveal Codes window and delete the overstrike code.

You can also use the characters in the WordPerfect character sets when creating an overstrike. To do this, press Ctrl-W in the Create Overstrike dialog box. Many commonly used overstrike characters are already available from the WordPerfect character sets.

● **SEE ALSO**   Font Attributes, Reveal Codes, WP Characters

PAGE BREAK

WordPerfect automatically inserts a *soft* page break at the bottom margin of each page, and adjusts the location of these soft page breaks as you edit. You can insert a *hard* page break anywhere on a page to make a new page begin at that location.

To Insert a Hard Page Break

1.   Position the cursor where you want to begin a new page.

2.   Press Ctrl-↵. Or, from the Layout menu, choose Alignment, and then choose Hard Page.

● **NOTES**   To delete a hard page break, display the Reveal Codes window and delete the code. Soft page breaks are displayed as single lines across the document window. Hard page breaks are displayed as double lines. When you are typing or editing columns, you can insert a hard page break to end a column and move the cursor to the top of the next column.

● **SEE ALSO**   Columns, Page Format, Reveal Codes

PAGE FORMAT

The Page Format command lets you modify some aspects of how text is formatted or printed on a page.

To Modify the Page Format

1.   Position the cursor on the page you want to modify.

2.   From the Layout menu, choose Page (Shift-F8,3).

3.   Change any of the options in the dialog box.

4.   Choose OK or press ↵.

Page Format Options

Page Numbering (1)   Lets you specify the type and
                            location for page numbering. See the
                            "Page Numbering" entry for more
                            information.

Center Page (2,3)   Centers text between the top and
                            bottom margins on the page. See the
                            "Center Page" entry for more
                            information.

Force Page (F)	Select **O**dd (1) or **E**ven (2) to make sure the current page is always an odd or even page. WordPerfect will insert a new page before the current one if necessary. Select **N**ew (3) to insert a hard page break at the location. See the "Page Break" entry for more information.
Paper Sizes (4-7)	Select a different paper size or type. See the "Paper Size" entry for more information.
Double-sided Printing (8)	If your printer can print double-sided pages, indicate whether it should rotate the paper around the long edge or short edge.
S**u**ppress (9)	Lets you suppress the printing of headers, footers, watermarks, and page numbering on the current page. Check all items you want to suppress in the dialog box and choose OK.
Delay Codes (D)	Lets you prevent selected formatting changes from being activated for a specified number of pages. You can delay codes, such as margin settings and font changes, that remain in effect once they are turned on, but you cannot delay paired, on/off codes, such as bolding and columns. Once you have specified the number of pages on which to delay codes, the Delay Codes window appears.
	To insert codes in the Delay Codes window, choose the commands from the menus and use the keystrokes as you normally do. The menu is still visible and active at the top of the screen. When you are finished, press F7 to close the window.

Page **B**orders (B)   Lets you add a border to the current
                              page. See the "Border" entry for
                              more information.

● **SEE ALSO**   Borders, Center Page, Page Break, Page Numbering, Paper Size

PAGE MODE

When you work in Page mode, WordPerfect tries to display each
page of your document—both the text and graphics—as close as
possible to how it will look when you print it. To do this, Word-
Perfect attempts to match the fonts and attributes with the available
display attributes. Page mode differs from Graphics mode in that,
in Page mode, headers, footers, footnotes, and endnotes are displayed.

To Work in Page Mode

Page mode is checked on the menu when active. To select it, from
the View menu choose Page mode (Ctrl-F3,4). Figure 13 shows the
main elements available for display when Page mode is active.

● **NOTES**   WordPerfect displays graphics in color even if you
have not selected a color printer. Use Graphics mode if you want to
display more of the body of your document while you are editing.
Use Print Preview if you want to see more than one page of your
document at a time prior to printing.

● **SEE ALSO**   Graphics Mode, Print Preview, Text Mode

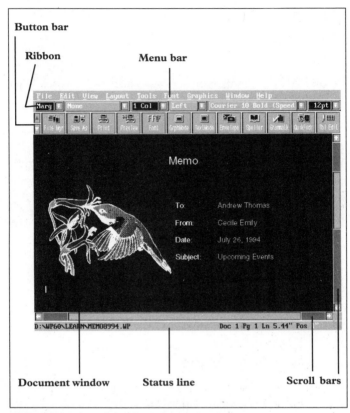

Figure 13: Elements of the Page mode window

PAGE NUMBERING

You can specify the type of page numbering you want and the location at which to print page numbers with the Page Numbering option in the Page Format dialog box. You can also print volume and chapter numbers.

To Number Pages

1. Position the cursor on the page where you want numbering to begin.

2. From the Layout menu, choose Page (Shift-F8,3).

3. Choose Page Numbering (1).

4. Select the position for the page number and choose OK. Refer to the right side of the dialog box to see where the page number will appear.

5. If you want to change the appearance of the page numbers, choose Font/Attributes/Color, make selections in the dialog box, and choose OK.

6. Choose OK or press ↵.

You can see the page numbers as they will look when printed by switching to Page mode (Ctrl-F3,4) or by using Print Preview (Shift-F7,7).

To Change the Page Number or Character

You can reset the page number or change the numbering method on any page.

1. Position the cursor on the page where you want the change to begin.

2. From the Layout menu, choose Page (Shift-F8,3).

3. Choose Page Numbering (1).

4. Choose Page Number (2)

5. Choose New Number (1), enter a new number in the text box, and press ↵.

6. Choose Numbering Method (2) and select a method from the pop-up list.

7. Choose OK or press ↵ until the document window is displayed.

To Suppress Page Numbering

1. Position the cursor on the page where you want to suppress the printing of a page number.

2. From the Layout menu, choose Page (Shift-F8,3).

3. Choose Suppress (9) and then select Page Numbering (7).

4. Choose OK or press ↵ until the document window is displayed.

● **NOTES**   The Chapter and Volume options in the Page Numbering dialog box let you also include chapter, volume, or section numbers in your document. They are inserted like page numbers but are not incremented automatically. Secondary page numbers can be included anywhere in your document; they are inserted like page numbers. Use the Insert Formatted Page Number option when you need to place the page number at the current cursor position.

● **SEE ALSO**   Font Attributes, Page Format

PAPER SIZE

The Paper Size/Type dialog box lets you select a different paper size for all or part of the current document. You can also create new paper definitions and edit those provided by WordPerfect. You must install and select the printer you will use before selecting a paper type.

To Specify the Paper Size

1. Position the cursor on the page where you want to select a different paper type.

2. From the Layout menu, choose Page (Shift-F8,3).

3. Choose Paper Size/Type (4).

4. Select the paper type from the Paper Name list box and choose Select (1). Refer to the Paper Details at the bottom of the dialog box for information about the paper type.

5. Choose OK or press ↵.

To Create or Edit a Paper Size Definition

You can create or edit a paper definition for the current printer, but it does not have to be used in the current document. It can be created at any time and selected when needed.

1. From the Layout menu, choose Page (Shift-F8,3).

2. Choose Paper Size/Type (4).

3. Highlight an item in the Paper Name list box and choose Create (2) or Edit (3). Select the most similar paper type if you are creating a new definition.

    • If you chose Create, type a name for the paper (for example, "Letterhead") in the Paper Name text box and press ↵.

4. Make a selection from the Paper Type (2) drop-down list box.

5. Choose Paper Size (3), if necessary, to change the paper size from the one shown. Highlight the correct setting in the list box and choose Select (1).

6. Select Paper Location (4), if necessary, to change the setting shown. Highlight the correct setting in the list box and choose Select (1).

7. Check Prompt to Load (5) if you want WordPerfect to prompt you to manually load a different paper type before printing.

8. Select Orientation (6), if necessary, to change the setting shown. Highlight the correct setting in the list box and choose OK.

9. To change the position at which text will print on the page, select Adjust Text (7). You can change the Top, Up or Down, or the Side, Left or Right position by typing a

number in the desired text box and pressing ↵. Change the numbers in the text boxes as needed.

10. When you've made the necessary changes, choose OK or press ↵ until you are back at the Page Format dialog box.

You can now select the paper you've defined or edited.

To Create Labels

WordPerfect provides definitions for many commercially produced labels. In most instances you only need to select the label type from those provided.

1. Position the cursor on the page where you want to begin creating labels.

2. From the Layout menu, choose **P**age (Shift-F8,3).

3. Choose **L**abels (5).

4. Highlight the label type in the Labels list box and choose **S**elect (1). Refer to the Label Details at the bottom of the dialog box for information about the label type.

5. If necessary, make changes in the Labels Printer Info dialog box, and then choose OK.

6. Choose OK or press ↵. If you used Shift-F8,3, press ↵ again to select close.

You can select another label type later in your document, if necessary.

Once you select a label definition, each label is shown on the screen separated by double lines when you are in Text mode or Graphic mode. Use Page mode or Print Preview to see how the labels will look when they are printed. If you print a single page when printing labels, only one label will be printed because WordPerfect treats each label as a separate page when printing. To print only specific labels, select them and print them as if each were a page in itself.

● **NOTES**   If you do not select a paper size and type, Word-Perfect uses the default paper definition, which is an 8 ½" × by 11" paper in portrait orientation.

If you want to define a paper type that can be used with all printers, select [ALL OTHERS] in the Paper Name list box. You are only asked to select a paper type and size, but you can edit [ALL OTHERS] to change other properties. Use [ALL OTHERS] if you intend to print a document on more than one printer after you create a new paper definition.

The selection in the Paper Size/Type dialog box affects the current document only. Change the paper size in Initial Codes Setup for it to affect all new documents.

● **SEE ALSO**   Envelopes, Graphics Mode, Initial Codes, Page Format, Page Mode, Print, Print Preview, Printer Select, Text Mode

PARAGRAPH NUMBERING

WordPerfect's outline feature lets you insert paragraph numbers in your document. You do not have to use the outline levels for the numbers.

To Number Paragraphs

1. Position the cursor where you want to begin numbering paragraphs.

2. From the Tools menu, choose Outline (Ctrl-F5).

3. Choose Begin New Outline (1).

4. In the list box, highlight the outline style you want to use and choose Select (1). These standard styles can be used for paragraph numbering:

Legal   Paragraphs numbered in the format
                 1, 1.1, 1.1.1

Legal 2	Paragraphs numbered in the format 1, 1.01, 1.01.01
Numbers	Paragraph numbering only, without levels
Paragraph	Numbers paragraphs in the format 1. a. i. (1) (a) (i)

5. Type the first paragraph and press ↵.

6. Add additional paragraphs with these techniques:

- To add another paragraph at the same number level as the previous one, type the text and press ↵.

- To add another paragraph at a subordinate level from the previous one, press Tab to move the next line in to the right an additional level, type the text, and press ↵.

- To add another paragraph at a higher level to the left of the previous one, press Shift-Tab to move the next line out one level, type the text, and press ↵.

7. Repeat steps 5 and 6 until you complete the document.

8. From the Tools menu, choose Outline and then choose End Outline (Ctrl-F5,5).

● **NOTES**   The Paragraph Number command available in previous versions of WordPerfect is no longer available. Use the Outline feature with the preceding steps instead to number paragraphs in a document.

● **SEE ALSO**   Line Numbering, Outline

PASSWORD

The Password feature lets you protect a file from being opened, retrieved, looked at, copied, moved, printed, or deleted from within WordPerfect. It does not protect files outside of WordPerfect, at the DOS prompt for example.

To Password-Protect a Document

To password-protect the current document:

1.   From the File menu, choose Save As (F10).

2.   Enter a name for the file in the Filename text box, but don't press ↵.

2.   Choose Password (F8).

3.   Enter the password in the text box and choose OK or press ↵.

4.   Enter the password again.

5.   Choose OK or press ↵.

6.   Choose OK or press ↵ to save the document with the password.

This technique lets you enter a new password or change the existing password. If you replace an existing password, you will see the prompt "Replace *filename*?" Choose Yes.

To Remove a Password

To remove the password from the current document, follow these steps:

1.   From the File menu, choose Save As (F10).

2.   Choose Password (F8).

3.   Choose Remove (F6).

4.   Choose OK or press ↵.

5.   Choose Yes to save the file without a password.

The password can only be removed from the current document.

• NOTES   A password can contain up to 23 alphanumeric characters and is not case-sensitive. Password-protection is automatically applied to any backup files associated with the document. When you save a password-protected file in another format besides WordPerfect, password protection is lost.

Password-protected files can be deleted from the DOS prompt. The level of security provided by WordPerfect passwords does not meet government or business high-level security standards.

- **SEE ALSO**   Save/Save As

PRINT

WordPerfect provides a number of print options that let you print all or part of the current document as well as any WordPerfect document on disk. The Print command also lets you cancel print jobs and review printer problems.

To Print a Document

1.   From the File menu, choose Print/Fax (Shift-F7).

2.   Select the part of the document (1–5) you want to print.

3.   Select and change any Output Options.

4.   Select and change any Document Settings.

5.   Choose Print.

Print Options

The following print settings and options are available in the Print Options dialog box.

Full Document (1)	Select this to print the current document.
Page (2)	Select this to print the current page.

Document on Disk (3)	Opens a dialog box where you can enter the file name and, if necessary, the path of the document to print. You can print any document on the hard disk or a floppy disk with this option.
Multiple Pages (4)	Opens a dialog box where you can select the pages to print. See Table 11 to enter a Page/Label Range. You can also print the document summary, print the document as a booklet, print in descending order, or print only odd or even pages.
Blocked Text (5)	Select this to print the currently selected (blocked) text.
Control Printer (6)	Opens a dialog box that displays information about printer activity and lets you prioritize and cancel jobs.
Print Preview (7)	Opens the Print Preview window for the current document.

Table 11: Sample Page/Label Range Entries

Enter	To Print
2	Page 2
2,4,6,11	Pages 2, 4, 6, and 11
2 11	Pages 2 and 11
2-	Page 2 through the end of the document
-11	The beginning of the document (page 1) through page 11
2-11	Page 2 through page 11
2-11 16	Page 2 through page 11 and page 16
2,4,6,11-16	Pages 2, 4, 6, and 11 through 16

Initialize Printer (8)	Downloads soft fonts after the printer is turned on.
Fax Services (9)	Opens a dialog box that lets you fax documents you've created in WordPerfect.
Print Job Graphically	Check this option when printing graphic images that have dark backgrounds behind light letters or graphics.
Number of Copies	Enter the number of copies of the current document you want to print.
Generated by	Choose whether to generate multiple copies by WordPerfect, the printer, or the network.
Output Options	Opens a dialog box for indicating how you want your print job to be sorted, grouped, or offset (available only if your printer supports these options).
Text Quality	Select the resolution and quality you want text printed at, if your printer can print at different resolutions. Draft quality will print the fastest.
Graphics Quality	Select the resolution and quality you want graphics printed at, if your printer can print at different resolutions. Draft quality will print the fastest.
Print Color	If a color printer is selected, select whether to print in color or with black ink only.

To Cancel a Print Job

1. From the File menu, choose Print/Fax (Shift-F7).

2. Choose Control Printer (6).

3. In the list box, highlight the print job you want to cancel, choose Cancel Job (1), and select Yes to confirm that you want to cancel the print job. All the jobs you have sent to the printer that have yet to be printed are on this list. To temporarily pause a job, highlight the job and choose Stop. Resume it later by highlighting it and choosing Go.

4. Choose Close.

● **NOTES** The Control Printer dialog box also displays status information about your printer. If you suspect there is a problem with a print job, choose Control Printer, look at the Status, and then try the Action.

● **SEE ALSO** Fax Services, Paper Size, Print Preview, Printer Select

Print Preview tries to display each page of your document—both the text and graphics—close to how it will look when you print it. Print Preview determines what to display based on the printer that is currently selected. You cannot edit your document in the Print Preview window, but you can review all the pages of a large document quickly and easily.

To Display the Print Preview Window

To open the Print Preview window, from the File menu choose Print Preview (Shift-F7,7). Figure 14 shows the main elements of the Print Preview window. Use the viewing options on the View menu and button bar to help review your document. When you are finished previewing your document, select File Close, or click the Close button to return to your document.

Print Preview button bar   Menu bar

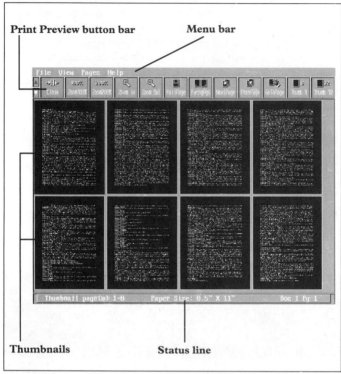

Thumbnails   Status line

Figure 14: The Print Preview window showing thumbnails

● **NOTES** WordPerfect displays graphic images even if the selected printer does not print them. The program displays color graphics in color even if you have not selected a color printer. To view graphics in black and white, choose Setup from the File menu in the Print Preview window, check View Text & Graphics in Black & White (1), and choose OK.

● **SEE ALSO** Go To, Page Mode, Printer Select, Zoom

PRINTER SELECT

Usually you choose one or more printers to install when you install WordPerfect. You can easily change the currently selected printer and select another installed printer. You can also add a printer to the list of installed printers in order to select it.

To Change the Selected Printer

1. From the File menu, choose Print/Fax (Shift-F7).
2. Choose Select.
3. Highlight a printer in the list box and choose Select (1).
4. Choose Close or press ⏎.

The printer selection is in effect for all new documents.

To Add a Printer

1. From the File menu, choose Print/Fax (Shift-F7).
2. Choose Select.
3. Choose Add Printer (2).
4. Highlight the printer you want to add in the list box and choose Select (1).
5. Choose OK to accept the Printer Filename as shown.
6. Read the information about the printer and choose Close or press ⏎.
7. Choose OK or press ⏎.
8. Choose Select (1) to select the highlighted printer.
9. Choose Close or press ⏎.

If the printer is not in the list of Available Printers in the Add Printer dialog box, use Other Dir (2) to display additional printers installed in another directory. If it is still not displayed, run the WordPerfect install program and select Custom Installation (2) in order to install the printer.

● **NOTES**   When you install a printer, WordPerfect copies an .ALL file to your computer with information about the installed printer and printers similar to it. Those similar printers are available and can be added; others must installed first in order to be added.

● **SEE ALSO**   Installing WordPerfect (in the Introduction), Print

QuickFinder creates special files so that WordPerfect can rapidly search for words and text strings. QuickFinder provides commands for creating, editing, updating, and searching through these files, called QuickFinder indexes. QuickFinder indexes include alphabetical listings of every word and text string in each indexed file, and information about the file(s) in which they appear.

QuickFinder indexes are not related to indexes you define and generate for your documents with the Index command.

To Create a QuickFinder Index

1.   From the File menu, choose File Manager (F5).
2.   Choose Use QuickFinder (F4).
3.   Choose Setup (Shift-F1).
4.   Choose Location of Files (6).
5.   Select either Personal Path (1) or Shared Path (2). Then, in the text box, type the directory path where you want WordPerfect to store your QuickFinder index files when they are created and press ↵. If you choose Shared Path,

your indexes can be used by other users on the network. If the directory has not been created, answer **Yes** to create the directory.

6. Choose OK or press ↵.

7. Choose **C**reate Index Definition (1).

8. Enter a useful description in the Index **D**escription (1) text box and press ↵.

9. Enter a different file name in the I**n**dex Filename (2) text box or accept the one shown and press ↵. WordPerfect will give the file an .IDX extension when it is created.

10. Choose **A**dd (1).

11. In the **F**ilename Pattern (1) text box, enter a directory path or a directory path and file name. The file name can include wildcards. This tells WordPerfect which files to include.

12. If you want all subdirectories in the directory included in the indexing, check **I**nclude Subdirectories (2), and then choose OK.

13. Press Esc and then choose **O**ptions (4), make any changes in the Options dialog box, and choose OK.

14. If you want WordPerfect to include additional directories or files in the indexing, choose Directories and Files to Index, and then repeat steps 10 through 14.

15. Choose OK or press ↵.

16. Choose Generate.

WordPerfect begins creating the index and displays its progress on-screen. When the index is finished, WordPerfect displays the Quick-Finder File Indexer dialog box, which lets you search for words and phrases.

17. You can close this dialog box by choosing OK. Or, follow the steps under "To Search a QuickFinder Index" to search the index now.

When you create subsequent indexes, you can skip steps 4 through 6 if you do not want to change the location of files.

QuickFinder Options

These options are available when creating or editing an index:

Level (1)	Select the level of detail to be included in the index, for example where the word appears.
Exclude Files (2)	Enter any files you want excluded from the search. You can use wild cards.
Index Document Text (3)	Select this option to only index the document text.
Index Document Summary (4)	Select this option to only index the summary text.
Index Both (5)	Select this option to index both the document text and summary.
Index WP Documents Only (6)	Check this option to include only WordPerfect documents in the indexing and ignore all others.
Include Numbers (7)	Check to include text strings with numbers in the indexing.
Manual Update Only (8)	Check to prevent this index from being automatically updated when you choose Update Indexes in the QuickFinder File Indexer dialog box.

To generate the index quickly, choose Document Level, select Index Document Text, and check Index WP Documents Only. Do not check Include Numbers.

To Search a QuickFinder Index

If the QuickFinder File Indexer dialog box is displayed because you have just finished creating an index, begin at step 3.

1. From the File menu, choose File Manager (F5).

2. Choose Use QuickFinder (F4).

3. Press Esc, select Index (1), enter the index you want to search or select it from the drop-down list box, and press ⏎.

4. Select Word Pattern (2), enter the text string you want to search for, and press ⏎. You can use operators in your search by choosing Operators, selecting from the list box, and choosing Insert. Table 12 explains the operators.

Table 12: QuickFinder Search Operators

Operator and Example	Use
And (&); smith & jones	Finds files that contain both words; the words do not have to appear together.
Or (¦); smith ¦ jones	Finds files that contain either or both words; the files must contain only one of the words to be indexed.
Not (-); smith - jones	Finds files that contain the first word but not the second word; files that contain the second word are not indexed.
Match Single Character (?); foo?	In this example, finds files that contain the characters *foo* followed by any single letter. Files with the words *food*, *fool*, and *foot* are indexed. The ? can appear anywhere in the word and can appear more than once.
Match Multiple Characters (*); b*t*	In this example, finds files with words that begin with *b* and contain a *t* and any additional letters (or no additional letters). Files with the words *bet*, *both*, *butter*, and *btu* are indexed. The * can appear anywhere in the word and can appear more than once.

5. Choose OK or press ↵. File Manager displays a list of files that contain the text string you enter. Other File Manager options are displayed at the bottom of the dialog box.

6. Highlight any file in the list and choose Look (3).

7. Choose Search (F2), enter the text string you want to search for in the text box, and choose Search again. Word-Perfect highlights the first occurrence of the text string. Use Search as many times as necessary to search through the file. Choose OK when you see the message "Not found," and then choose Close.

8. Repeat steps 6 and 7 for each file and each text string you want to search through.

9. Choose Close to return to the document window.

● **NOTES**   When indexing the specified files and directories, QuickFinder includes documents in WordPerfect 4.2, 5.0, 5.1, and 6.0 format. It ignores open, temporary, password-protected, executable, and other index files.

After you edit some of your indexed files, you can generate the index again or use the Update Indexes button in the QuickFinder File Indexer dialog box to update the index. Updating an index is faster, but updated indexes require more disk space than newly generated ones.

● **SEE ALSO**   File Manager, Search, Setup

The QuickList is a list of the files you use most often, organized by type. It can help you open the directory listing associated with the

file type, open a specific file, and enter a directory and/or file name in a dialog box.

To Create Your QuickList

1. From the File menu, choose File Manager (F5).
2. Choose QuickList (F6).
3. Choose Create (2).
4. Enter a useful description in the Description (1) text box and press ⏎.
5. Enter the directory path in the Filename/Directory (2) text box and press ⏎. You can also include a file specification with the wild cards ? and *.
6. Choose OK or press ⏎.
7. Repeat steps 3 through 6 to add other directories to your list.

The description you enter is displayed in the list box. When you highlight the description, the Filename/Directory entry is shown at the top of the dialog box.

To Edit Your QuickList

1. From the File menu, choose File Manager (F5).
2. Choose QuickList (F6).
3. In the list box, highlight an entry you want to remove and choose Delete (4).
4. Highlight an entry you want to modify and choose Edit (3).
5. Make any changes in the Description (1) and Filename/Directory (2) text boxes.
6. Choose OK or press ⏎, and then select Close to close the QuickList, and OK to display the File Manager. Select Close to return to your document.

To Use the QuickList

The QuickList button is available from dialog boxes where you have to enter a file name. For example, the Open, Retrieve, and Save As dialog boxes all offer the Quicklist button. To use the QuickList from any dialog box:

1.   Choose QuickList (F6).

2.   From here you have two options:

- In the list box, highlight the item you want to open and choose Select (1). If the item you select is a directory, File Manager is opened with the contents of that directory. See the "File Manager" entry for more information.

- In the list box, highlight the item you want to insert in the Filename/Directory text box in the current dialog box and choose Use as Pattern (5).

• **NOTES**   If the Setup option Update QuickList is checked, there will already be items in the list, based on the directories entered in the Setup Location of Files dialog box.

• **SEE ALSO**   File Manager, Open, Retrieve, Save/Save As, Setup

REDLINING
AND STRIKEOUT

Redlining is used to mark text that has been added to a document; strikeout marks text that has been deleted.

To Insert Redlining or Strikeout

1. If you haven't yet typed the text, position the cursor where you want to begin the redlining or strikeout. If you've already entered the text, select (block) the text you want to mark.

2. From the Font menu, choose **R**edline or **S**trikeout.

3. When you finish typing the text, repeat step 2.

To Change the Redlining Method

1. From the Layout menu, choose **D**ocument (Shift-F8,4).

2. Select an option from the **R**edline Method (5) pop-up list. **P**rinter Dependent causes most printers to print redlined text with a shaded box behind it. **L**eft, **R**ight, or **A**lternating places a character in the margin.

3. If you select **L**eft, **R**ight, or **A**lternating, choose Redline Character (6) to change the character from a vertical bar (|) to another character. Type a character in the text.

4. Choose OK or press ↵. If you used (Shift-F8,4), choose Close or press ↵.

To Remove Redlining and Strikeout

To remove all the markings in a document:

1. From the File menu, choose Compare **D**ocuments, and choose **R**emove Markings (Alt-F5,9).

2. Select **R**emove Redline Markings and Strikeout Text (1) and press ↵.

To remove markings from a specific block of text, display the Reveal Codes window and delete the Redline or Strikeout code.

• **NOTES** You can enter a special character in the Redline Character text box by pressing Ctrl-W to open the WordPerfect character dialog box.

• **SEE ALSO** Compare Documents, WP Characters

With Repeat, you can have WordPerfect automatically repeat a keystroke, command, or macro. Examples of commands and keys that can be repeated are cursor movement keys, letters, numbers, symbols, and delete.

To Repeat Operations

1. From the Edit menu, choose Repeat (Ctrl-R).

2. Enter the number of times you want to repeat the keystroke or command in the Count text box.

3. Then press the key. Or, press Alt-F10 and select the macro you want to repeat.

Or, enter the number you want to be the next default count, press ↵, and choose Set.

• **NOTES** To cancel a macro in progress, press Esc or Ctrl-Break.

• **SEE ALSO** Delete, Macros, and the inside front cover of the book for Cursor Movement Keys

REPLACE

Replace lets you automatically replace a word, text string, or code with another that you specify. You can replace every occurrence or only a specific occurrence.

To Replace Text

1. Position the cursor where you want to begin the replacement.

2. From the Edit menu, choose Replace (Alt-F2).

3. In the Search For (1) text box, enter the word or text string you want to replace and press ↵.

You can also choose Specific Codes (Shift-F5), highlight a code in the list box, and choose Select.

4. In the Replace With (2) text box, enter the word or text string you want to replace it with and press ↵. To delete all occurrences of the text, leave <Nothing> in the text box.

5. Select any options (see "Replace Options").

6. Choose Replace (F2).

7. Choose OK or press ↵ when you see the Search and Replace Complete dialog box.

To Search for Codes

1. Position the cursor where you want to begin the replacement.

2. From the Edit menu, choose Replace (Alt-F2).

3. With the cursor in the Search For text box, choose Codes (F5), highlight a code in the list box, and choose Select.

   You can also choose Specific Codes (Shift-F5), highlight a code in the list box, and choose Select. Then enter information in the additional dialog box and choose OK. Next, follow the previous steps 6 and 7.

4.   With the cursor in the Replace With text box, choose
Codes (F5), highlight a code in the list box, and choose
Select. To delete all occurrences of the code, leave
<Nothing> in the text box.

5.   Select any options.

6.   Choose Replace (F2).

7.   Choose OK or press ↵ when you see the Search and
Replace Complete dialog box.

Replace Options

Confirm Replacement (3)	The Confirm Replacement dialog box is displayed and the first occurrence is highlighted in the document window. Choose Yes to replace the text or No to skip it. If you want WordPerfect to replace the text and stop asking you for confirmation, choose Replace All.
Backward Search (4)	Searches backward from the current cursor position.
Case Sensitive Search (5)	Only words or text strings that match exactly the case entered in the Search For text box are found and replaced.
Find Whole Words Only (6)	Only whole words or text strings that match exactly those entered in the Search For text box are found and replaced. Variations of the entry are ignored.
Extended Search (7)	WordPerfect also searches outside the body of the document—for example, in the headers, footers, footnotes, endnotes, and comments—for the word, text string, or code.

Limit Number of
Matches (8)

Enter a number in the text box to
place a limit on the number of times
the word, text string, or code can be
replaced.

● **NOTES** You can enter a special character in the Search For text
box by pressing Ctrl-W to open the WordPerfect character dialog
box. You can enter wildcard characters in the Search For text box by
choosing Codes (F5) and selecting ? or * from the list box. You can
replace text and codes at the same time by entering both in the Search
For text box.

● **SEE ALSO** Search, WP Characters

RETRIEVE

The Retrieve command lets you open an existing document and insert it into the current document at the position of the cursor. Use it
if you currently have a document open and want to insert or append the contents of another document in or to it.

To Retrieve a Document

1. From the File menu, choose Retrieve.

2. In the Filename (1) text box, enter the path and file name
   of the file you want to retrieve. If the file is located in the
   default directory, you only need to enter the file name. You
   can also highlight a file name from the drop-down list, or
   use File Manager (F5) or QuickList (F6) to select the file.

3. Choose OK or press ↵.

If you change your mind and want to retrieve the document into a
new document window, select Open into New Document (1) as the
Method (2) in the Retrieve Document dialog box before choosing OK.

• **NOTES**   WordPerfect can retrieve files created with many other applications, so that you can edit them in WordPerfect 6.0. See the entry under "Open" for more information.

• **SEE ALSO**   Append, File Manager, New, Open, QuickList, Setup

REVEAL CODES

The Reveal Codes window lets you see the hidden codes Word-Perfect inserts when you make format changes and other entries throughout a document.

To Use the Reveal Codes Window

When active, Reveal Codes is checked or starred on the menu and the Reveal Codes window is displayed in the lower half of the screen. To open the window, from the View menu choose Reveal Codes (Alt-F3). To close it at any time, choose Reveal Codes (Alt-F3) again. Figure 15 shows the main elements of the Reveal Codes window.

The Reveal Codes Window

The Reveal Codes window shows the text in the document and all the codes. Codes are displayed with square brackets. Depending on your current viewing mode and color selections, codes may also be displayed in a contrasting color or as highlighted text. Table 1 (in the "Codes" entry) lists WordPerfect codes and their meanings.

The cursor is displayed according to your setup for blocked text, usually a rectangle in reverse video. As you move the cursor through the document, it moves through the Reveal Codes window below. The divider line between the two parts of the window shows the tab stops.

Cursor   Document window

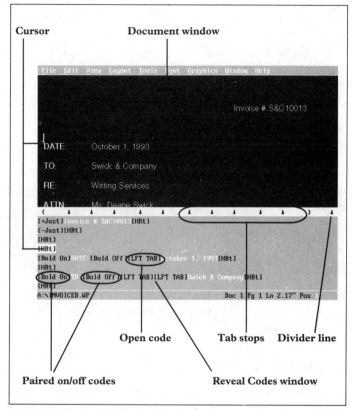

Open code   Tab stops   Divider line

Paired on/off codes   Reveal Codes window

Figure 15: The Reveal Codes window

To Delete a Code

Place the cursor over the code and press Delete. When deleting paired codes, you only have to delete one of the pair; WordPerfect deletes the other.

To Move or Copy a Code

1. Select (block) the code and any text you want to include.

2. From the Edit menu, choose either Copy and Paste (Ctrl-Ins) or Cut and Paste (Ctrl-Del).

3. Move the cursor to the new location and press ↵.

● **NOTES** To change the size of the Reveal Codes window, Choose Screen Setup from the View menu.

● **SEE ALSO** Codes, Copy/Copy and Paste, Cut/Cut and Paste/Move, Delete, Initial Codes, Screen Setup, Select, Setup

The Ribbon provides quick access to several WordPerfect display and formatting features. The Ribbon can only be used in conjunction with a mouse.

To Use the Ribbon

To display the Ribbon, from the View menu choose **R**ibbon. When the Ribbon is active, it is checked or starred on the menu. The Ribbon, as displayed in Graphics and Page modes, is shown in Figure 16. You can turn off the Ribbon display at any time by choosing **R**ibbon again from the **V**iew menu.

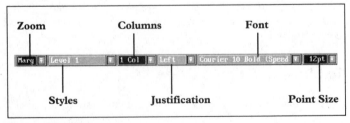

Figure 16: The Ribbon

The Ribbon provides access to the following features:

Zoom	Lets you change the displayed size of text and graphics in the document window. Zoom is not available in Text mode.
Styles	Lets you change the style of all or selected paragraphs. When creating an outline, you can also change the outline style.
Columns	Lets you divide all or part of the document into newspaper-style columns.
Justification	Lets you change the justification for all or selected paragraphs.
Font	Lets you change the font for the entire document or selected (blocked) text.
Point Size	Lets you change the point size for the entire document or selected (blocked) text.

Click the prompt button to open the drop-down list box and display the available selections. Then double-click your choice. Changes affect the current document only. All but Zoom can be applied either to all text after the change or to selected text only. Zoom affects the way a document is displayed but has no affect on how it is printed. See the individual entries for more information on each feature. See the "Font" entry for more information about point size.

● **NOTES** Use Screen Setup on the View menu to have the Ribbon always displayed when you start WordPerfect.

● **SEE ALSO** Columns, Font, Justification, Outline, Screen Setup, Styles, Zoom

SAVE/SAVE AS

The Save command saves the current version of the document and replaces the document of the same name that is stored on the hard disk. The Save As command saves the current document under a file name you specify. If you save an existing document with a new name, the old version of that document remains on the hard disk.

To Save and Name a Document

1. From the File menu, choose Save As (F10).

2. Enter a file name in the Filename text box (1). You can save an existing document under a new name by replacing its name in the text box.

3. If you want to save the document in a format other than WordPerfect 6.0, open the Format (2) drop-down list and make a selection. The document will be converted to that format.

4. Choose OK or press ↵.

File names can have up to eight characters and a one- to three-character extension following a period, such as *filename.ext*. Files are saved in the default path specified in Setup Location of Files, unless you also enter a path in the Filename text box.

To Save a Revised Document

To save a document that you've already named, from the File menu choose Save (Ctrl-F12). If you choose Save for an unnamed document, the Save As dialog box is displayed.

● **NOTES**   Documents remain open after you save them. If you choose Close or one of the Exit commands, WordPerfect prompts you to save any open modified documents.

● **SEE ALSO**   Exit Document/Exit WP/Close, Password, Setup

Screen Setup lets you change the default setting for many objects WordPerfect displays.

To Set Up Screen Defaults

1. From the View menu, choose Screen Setup (Ctrl-F3, Shift-F1).

2. Change any option settings in this dialog box (see "Setup Options"). Check any objects you want displayed when you start WordPerfect, or remove the check from any you don't want displayed.

3. When you are finished, choose OK.

Setup Options

Some options are applied in all viewing modes. Others have (Graphics) or (Text) next to them to indicate the mode where they will be in effect. Graphics settings are applied in Graphics and Print modes.

Screen Options (1)	Select whether to display the menu bar, ribbon, outline bar, and button bar, choose a button bar and button bar options, and allow the Alt key to open the menus.
Display Characters (2)	Enter a character to be displayed on-screen when there is a hard return or space in the document. WP characters can be used.
Display of Merge Codes (3)	Select whether to show or hide codes or to display them as icons when inserting merge codes in a document.

Window Options (4)	Select whether to display the window frames, scroll bars, or comments, and specify what should be displayed in the left portion of the status bar.
Reveal Codes (5)	Specify whether to display details within the codes in the Reveal Codes window, and the size of the Reveal Codes window.
Zoom (6)	Select or specify the degree of magnification for text and graphics displayed in the document window.

● **NOTES**   You can enter special characters in the Display Characters text boxes by pressing Ctrl-W to open the WordPerfect character dialog box.

● **SEE ALSO**   Button Bar, Comments, Menus, Merge, Outline Bar, Reveal Codes, Ribbon, Scroll Bars, Windows, Zoom

Use the horizontal and vertical scroll bars to display a part of the document that is not visible on the screen. The scroll bars can only be used in conjunction with a mouse.

To Display and Use the Scroll Bars

1.   From the **V**iew menu, choose **H**orizontal Scroll Bar.

2.   From the **V**iew menu, choose **V**ertical Scroll Bar.

Scroll bars contain buttons with arrows at each end and a scroll box between the arrow buttons.

- Click ↑ or ↓ to move the cursor one line up or down.

- Click above or below the scroll box on the vertical scroll bar to first move the cursor one screen up or down and to then scroll one screen up or down.

- Click to the left or right of the scroll box on the horizontal scroll bar to first move the cursor one screen to the left or right and to then scroll one screen to the left or right.

- Click and hold the ↑, ↓, ←, or → to scroll freely in that direction.

- Click and drag the scroll box on either scroll bar to access an approximate location in the document. For example, if you drag the scroll box to the middle of the vertical scroll bar, you'll display the middle of your document.

● **NOTES**   The default setting for horizontal and vertical scroll bars is set in the Screen Setup dialog box. Scroll bars are also available in many dialog boxes and are used to scroll through a list of selections. Cursor movement keys also let you reposition the cursor within a document and can be used in conjunction with or instead of scroll bars.

● **SEE ALSO**   Screen Setup, and the inside front cover for Cursor Movement Keys

SEARCH

Search moves the cursor to the next occurrence in your current document of a word, text string, or code that you specify.

To Search for Text

1.   Position the cursor where you want to begin the search.

2. From the Edit menu, choose Search (F2).

3. In the Search For (1) text box, enter the word or text string you want to move the cursor to.

4. Select any options. See the entry under "Replace" for a description of the Search options.

5. Choose Search (F2).

6. To search again, choose Search from the Edit menu, and then choose Search in the dialog box (F2,F2).

To Search for Codes

1. Position the cursor where you want to begin the search.

2. From the Edit menu, choose Search (F2).

3. Choose Codes (F5), highlight a code in the list box, and choose Select. You can also choose Specific Codes (Shift-F5), highlight a code in the list box, choose Select, enter information in the additional dialog box, and choose OK.

4. Follow the previous steps 4 through 6.

• **NOTES**   You can enter a special character in the Search For text box by pressing Ctrl-W to open the WP Character dialog box. You can enter wildcard characters in the Search For text box by choosing Codes (F5) and selecting ? or * from the list box. You can search for text and codes at the same time by entering both in the Search For text box.

• **SEE ALSO**   Replace, WP Characters

SELECT

Use the Select command to select a sentence, paragraph, page, tabular column, or rectangular section of text for subsequent action. You can also select with the mouse.

To Select with the Select Command

The Sentence, Paragraph, and Page options lets you quickly select and block text to be acted upon.

1.   Position the cursor in the sentence, paragraph, or page you want to select.

2.   From the Edit menu, choose Select.

3.   Select Sentence, Paragraph, or Page.

Use the Tabular Column option to move, copy, or delete part or all of a column. Tabular columns are columns separated by tabs or indents. Use Rectangle to select a block of text that is set off with spaces.

1.   Block the section of the column you want to select.

2.   From the Edit menu, choose Select.

3.   Select Tabular Column or Rectangle.

4.   Select the desired action from the dialog box. If you are pasting the selection, move the cursor and press ↵.

To Select with a Mouse

• Double-click to select the current word.

• Triple-click to select the current sentence.

• Quadruple-click to select the current paragraph.

● **NOTES**   To cancel a selection, press Esc. To undelete text you've selected and deleted, choose Undelete from the Edit menu. To save text you've selected, choose Save As from the File menu.

● **SEE ALSO**   Block, Cancel, Save/Save As, Undelete

SETUP

Setup lets you change the default settings for file locations and the way your mouse, display, and keyboard are configured to run with WordPerfect. You can also create and edit color palettes and specify your preferences for some WordPerfect features.

To Modify Mouse Settings

WordPerfect usually selects the correct mouse driver during installation. If you are using a mouse with WordPerfect and are having problems, select the mouse driver with these steps. You can also modify the current mouse settings.

1.   From the File menu, choose Setup and then choose Mouse (Shift-F1,1).

2.   Choose Type (1).

3.   Highlight the correct mouse driver in the list box and choose Select (1). If you are using a Serial mouse, you'll also have to select the correct port in the Port pop-up box.

4.   Change any option settings, as follows:

Double-click Interval (3)	If WordPerfect is not responding when you double-click, increase the amount of time in the text box.
Acceleration Factor (4)	Change the number to increase or decrease WordPerfect's response when you move the mouse.
Left-handed Mouse (5)	Check to reverse the functioning of the left and right mouse buttons if you are clicking the mouse with your left hand.

5. Choose OK or press ↵. If you used (Shift-F1,1), you'll have to select Close.

To Modify Display Settings

WordPerfect lets you select the display driver during installation. If you are having problems, select a different driver. You can also modify the colors used for display with these steps.

1. From the File menu, choose Setup and then choose Display (Shift-F1,2).

2. Choose either Graphics Mode Screen Type/Colors (1) or Text Mode Screen Type/Colors (2).

3. Choose Screen Type (1).

4. Highlight the correct type in the list box and choose Select (1). Then highlight the correct screen resolution and choose Select (1). Alternately, let WordPerfect select the correct screen type by choosing Auto Select (2).

5. Highlight the color scheme in the list box and choose Select (1). To choose a different color scheme, select Color Schemes (2).

6. Choose Close or press ↵. If you used (Shift-F1,2) you'll have to select Close again.

The Graphics Mode Screen Type/Colors settings are used for both Graphics and Page modes.

To Modify Environment Settings

The options in the Environment dialog box let you indicate your preferences for many WordPerfect features.

1. From the File menu, choose Setup and then choose Environment (Shift-F1,3).

2. Choose any options and change the settings. Some options display additional dialog boxes (see "Environment Options").

3.   When you have finished changing options, choose OK or press ↵. If you used (Shift-F1,3), you must also select Close or press ↵ again.

Environment Options

Backup Options (1)	Have WordPerfect perform automatic backups options. See the entry under "Backup."
B**e**ep Options (2)	If you want WordPerfect to alert you with a beep sound on an error, hyphenation and/or search failure, choose this option, check the desired boxes, and choose OK.
Cursor Speed (3)	Select another setting to increase or decrease WordPerfect's response when you press the arrow keys.
Allow Undo (4)	Check this option if you want to use the Undo command to undo editing or formatting in the document window. Some operations take more time when Undo is allowed.
Format Document for Default Printer on Open (5)	Check this option if you want WordPerfect to reformat every document you open for the currently selected printer. If not checked, WordPerfect tries to select the printer that was selected when the document was saved.
Prompt for Hyphenation (6)	Have WordPerfect prompt you before hyphenating. See the entry under "Hyphenation."

Units of Measure (7)	Choose this option if you want to change the way WordPerfect displays and you enter numbers. Select any available settings from the pop-up boxes and choose OK. See the entry under "Units of Measure."
Language (L)	Lets you select a language that will be applied to all new documents. See the entry under "Language."
WordPerfect 5.1 Keyboard (K)	Check this option if you want the Escape, F1, and F3 keys to operate as they did with WordPerfect 5.1. When checked, press Escape to repeat, F1 to cancel, and F3 for help.
Auto Code Placement (T)	Causes WordPerfect to place certain formatting codes at the beginning of the paragraph or page, no matter where you insert them in the document. See the entry under "Auto Code Placement."
WordPerfect 5.1 Cursor Movement (W)	Check this option if you want the cursor movement keys to operate as they did with WordPerfect 5.1. See "Cursor Movement Keys" on the inside front cover.
Delimited Text Options (D)	Lets you identify the characters or codes you used to define fields and records in order to merge ASCII-delimited text files. See the entry under "Merge."

To Select an Alternate Keyboard Layout

You can select, create, and modify keyboard definitions with the Keyboard Layout feature. A keyboard definition is made up of the full set of operations associated with every key. Four keyboard definitions are included with WordPerfect: CUA, Equation, Macros, and Original.

1. From the File menu, choose Setup and choose Keyboard Layout (Shift-F1,4).

2. Highlight another keyboard in the list box and choose Select (1).

3. Choose OK or press ↵ until all the dialog boxes are closed.

To Create or Modify a Keyboard Layout

1. From the File menu, choose Setup and choose Keyboard Layout (Shift-F1,4).

2. In the list box, highlight the name of the keyboard you want to modify, and choose Edit (3). (You cannot edit the original keyboard.) You can also choose Create (2), enter a new name in the text box, and press ↵.

3. To add a command or macro, choose Create (1). Or, to modify an existing keystroke, highlight it in the list box, choose Edit (2), and skip to step 5.

4. Press the keystrokes to which you want to assign the command or macro in order to enter them in the Key (1) text box.

5. Enter a description in the Description (2) text box, if you wish, and press ↵.

6. Select Command (4). Or select Macro (5), select Retrieve Macro (2), and enter the name of the macro in the list box.

7. Choose OK or press ↵.

8. Repeat steps 3 through 7 for each keystroke you want to add.

9. Choose OK or press ↵ until all the dialog boxes are closed.

To Specify the Default Location of Files

The Location of Files dialog box shows the drive and directory where WordPerfect expects to find certain types of files and where it saves those files when you enter only a file name. If you are using WordPerfect on a network, you can indicate a Shared Directory for the files that co-workers need to access.

1. From the File menu, choose Setup, and choose Location of Files (Shift-F1,5).

2. Select the options you want to change. Some options open additional dialog boxes with two or more text boxes.

3. In each text box, enter the full path of the directory and press ↵. You can use the Directory Tree (F8) or QuickList (F6) to enter directory paths.

4. To change the location of Graphics Fonts Data Files, choose this option, highlight a font type in the list box, and choose Edit Path (1). Then enter the full path of the directory and press ↵.

5. Select OK in the Graphics Fonts Data Files dialog box.

6. To have the QuickList updated to reflect your changes, check Update QuickList.

The default location of these file types can be changed: Backup Files (1), Macros/Keyboards/Button Bar (2), Writing Tools (3), Printer Files (4), Style Files (5), Graphics Files (6), Documents (7), Spreadsheet Files (8), QuickFinder Files (9), WP.DRS and *.WFW Files (R), and Screen Font Data Files (S).

WP.DRS and *.WFW Files are used when you choose Print Preview or try to print WP characters graphically.

If you change the location of any files in this dialog box, make sure you also move those files to the new directory so that WordPerfect can find them.

To Select another Color Palette

If you are going to be printing in color, you may want to select, modify, or create a color palette with this feature.

1. From the File menu, choose Setup and choose Color Palette or Color Printing Palette (Shift-F1,6).

2. Highlight another palette in the list box and choose Select (1).

3. Choose OK or press ↵ until all the dialog boxes are closed.

To Create or Modify a Color Palette

1. From the File menu, choose Setup and choose Color Palette or Color Printing Palette (Shift-F1,6).

2. You can create a new palette or edit an existing one:

   • To create a new palette, choose Create (2), enter a name for the palette, and press ↵. Highlight it in the list box and choose Edit (3).

   • To edit an existing palette, highlight it in the list box and choose Edit (3).

3. To create a new color, choose Create (1), enter a name in the Color Name (1) text box, and press ↵.

4. Enter the Red, Green, and Blue values, or move the marker in the color wheel and luminosity bar to define the color. Then select OK or press ↵.

5. To modify a color, highlight the color and choose Edit (3).

6. Change the Red, Green, and Blue values, or drag the marker with the mouse in the color wheel and luminosity bar to define the color.

7. Choose OK or Delete until all the dialog boxes are closed.

● **SEE ALSO**   Auto Code Placement, Backup, File Manager, Hyphenation, Language, Macros, Merge, Printer Select, Quick-Finder, QuickList, Save/Save As, Undo, Units of Measure.

SORT AND SELECT

The Sort command lets you sort text alphabetically or numerically. It also lets you select specific records or text from a table or document.

To Sort a Document or Records

To sort an entire document, follow these steps. If you need to sort a table within the current document, position the cursor within the table before beginning the following steps.

1. From the Tools menu, choose Sort (Ctrl-F9,2).

2. Select the document you want to sort. You can select Document on Screen (1), the default, or File (2). If you select a file type, type the file name and, if necessary, the path in the File text box, and press ↵.

3. Select the destination of the sort. You can select Document on Screen (3), the default, or File (4). If you select a different file, type the file name and, if necessary, the path in the File text box. Then press ↵.

4. Choose OK or press ↵.

5. Select a different Record Type (1) to sort by in the pop-up list, if necessary. See "Records and Fields Options."

6. Add or Edit the Sort Keys (2) if necessary. See "To Set the Sort Priority."

7. Check Sort Uppercase First (5) if you want WordPerfect to sort uppercase letters first. Otherwise, lowercase letters will be sorted first.

8. Choose Perform Action.

To sort part of a document or table, follow these steps:

1. Select (block) the text you want to sort.

2. From the Tools menu, choose Sort (Ctrl-F9).

3. Follow the previous steps 4 through 7.

Records and Fields Options

WordPerfect can sort five types of records, defined as follows:

Merge Data File	Contains fields, lines, and words; ends with an ENDRECORD code.

Parallel Column	Contains columns, lines, and words; each row of columns is treated as a record.
Table	Contains cells, lines, and words; each row of cells is treated as a record.
Line	Contains fields and words; ends with a hard return.
Paragraph	Contains fields, lines, and words; ends with at least two hard returns.

In merge data files, fields end in ENDFIELD codes. In normal text, each line is considered a field, unless tabs and indents are inserted. Tabs and indents separate a line into additional fields.

To Set the Sort Priority

The Sort priority is set by creating one or more *keys* that tell Word-Perfect which part of the record (line, field, word) to sort by first, which part to sort by next, and so on. For example, you can sort by the third word in the second line by entering Line 2 and Word 3 for Key1 in the Edit Sort Key dialog box.

When the Sort dialog box is open, follow these steps to set the sort priority:

1.   Choose Sort **K**eys (2).

2.   Choose one of the Key options:

Add (1)	Add a new key.
Edit (2)	Modify the highlighted key.
Delete (3)	Delete the highlighted key.
Insert (4)	Insert a new key before the highlighted key and renumber the keys.

3.   Change any options in the Edit Sort Key dialog box. To define by the last cell or word in a line, or the last line in a paragraph, enter −1 for that item and press ↵.

4.   Repeat steps 2 and 3 to define up to nine sort keys.

5.   When you are finished, choose OK. Then continue with the steps under "To Sort a Record."

To Extract Records

To extract records from an entire document, follow these steps:

1.   From the Tools menu, choose Sort (Ctrl-F9,2).

2.   To sort the current document, select Document on Screen (1), the default, as the source. To select a different document to sort, select File (2) as the source. Then type the source, type the name of the file, and, if necessary, its path. Then press ⏎.

3.   To have the sort results appear in the current document, choose Document on Screen (3), the default, as the destination. To have the results of the sort sent to a different file, select File (4) as the destination. Then type in the name and, if necessary, the path of the file and press ⏎.

4.   Select OK or press ⏎.

5.   Choose Select Records (3) and type the selection criteria in the text box and press ⏎. For example, to find all records that contain a certain word, use the global key *keyg* with an equal sign, as in *keyg=anyword*. You can define up to nine keys. See "Record Selection" for more information.

6.   Check Select Without Sorting (4) if you want to extract information only and do not want to sort the rest of the text.

7.   Choose Perform Action.

To extract from part of a document or table, follow these steps:

1.   Select (block) the text you want to select from.

2.   From the Tools menu, choose Sort (Ctrl-F9,2).

3.   Follow the previous steps 4 through 6.

Record Selection

You select records by entering "key" statements to prioritize how you want the selection to proceed. Use the global key, *keyg*, and key1 through key9 in a statement combined with the operators in Table 13. You can separate each key statement with a comma, like so:

key1=NY,key2=1993

Table 13: Sort Operators

Operator	Usage
AND (&)	Selects records that match the conditions of both keys. Example: key1=1993 & key2=1994
OR (¦)	Selects records that match the conditions of either key. Example: key1=1993 ¦ key2=1994
=	Selects records that match the key. Example: key1=Alaska.
<>	Selects records that do not match the key. Example: key1<>Alaska.
>	Selects records that have greater numerical or alphabetical information than that specified in a key. Example: key2>6,000.
<	Selects records that have lesser numerical or alphabetical information than that specified in a key. Example: key2<6,000.
>=	Selects records that have greater numerical or alphabetical information than that specified in a key or that match the key. Example: key3>=Mississippi.
<=	Selects records that have lesser numerical or alphabetical information than that specified in a key or that match the key. Example: key3<=Michigan.

● **NOTES**   Before you begin any sort or select procedure, it's always best to save your document. If a sort or select operation does not produce the desired results, choose Undo from the Edit menu (Ctrl-Z) to reverse the action. When sorting text, codes are sorted

with the lines in which they occur. Whenever possible, use Document Initial Codes to move codes outside the text before sorting.

● **SEE ALSO**   Initial Codes, Merge, Save/Save As, Tables, Undo

This entry describes how to add a sound clip to a document and play it back. You must have a sound card or similar device installed in your computer to use sound clips.

To Set Up a Sound Device

When you installed WordPerfect, you were asked if you wanted to install a sound device. Once you've installed the sound device, follow these steps to set it up.

1.   From the Tools menu, choose Sound Clip, and then choose Sound Setup (Ctrl-F7,5, Shift-F1).

2.   Choose Type (1). In the list box, highlight the sound device installed on your system and choose Select (1).

3.   If you've changed the manufacturer's hardware settings for your device, choose Hardware Setup (2), make the necessary changes in the dialog box, and choose OK.

4.   Choose OK or Close until all dialog boxes are closed.

To Add Sound to a Document

1.   From the Tools menu, choose Sound Clip and then choose Add or Add Clip (Ctrl-F7,5,1).

2.   Enter the Filename (1) of the sound clip and press ↵.

3. If you wish, enter a Description (2) for the sound clip and press ↵.

4. Select Link to File on Disk (3) if the document's sound clip will be played back from the current hard disk or if the sound clip is stored on a shared network path. The document size will remain the same. Or, select Store in Document (4) if the document's sound clip is going to be played back from another location. The file will be much larger with the sound clip included.

5. Choose OK or Close until all dialog boxes are closed.

To Play a Sound Clip

1. From the Tools menu, choose Sound Clip, and then choose Play (Ctrl-F7,5).

2. Highlight a sound clip in the Clip Description list box and choose Play/Pause.

3. When you are finished, choose OK or Close until all dialog boxes are closed.

● **NOTES** Two types of sound files can be used with WordPerfect: musical instrument digital interface (MIDI) and digital audio. If you have the necessary hardware, you can also record sound with digital audio files.

SPELLER

The Speller can be used to check your document for misspellings and some common typing errors, including duplicate words and irregular capitalization.

To Spell-Check a Document

1. Position the cursor anywhere in the document.

2. From the Tools menu, choose Writing Tools (Alt-F1).

3. Choose Speller (1).

4. Choose the portion of the document whose spelling you want to check:

Word (1)	Only the current word is checked.
Page (2)	Only the current page is checked.
Document (3)	The document is checked from beginning to end.
From Cursor (4)	The document is checked from the cursor to the end.

WordPerfect highlights the first unknown word in the document and presents a list of suggested replacements.

5. Highlight a replacement in the list box and choose Replace Word (7), or double-click the replacement. If an appropriate replacement is not displayed, choose one of the other options:

Skip Once (1)	Leaves the word as-is but displays it the next time it occurs.
Skip in this Document (2)	Leaves the word as-is and ignores it if it occurs again.
Add to Dictionary (3)	Leaves the word as-is and adds it to the speller dictionary so it will not be displayed as an error anymore.
Edit Word (4)	Returns you to your document window. Edit the word and press F7 to continue checking.
Lookup (5)	Displays words that match phonetically, although spelled differently.
Ignore Numbers (6)	When checked, WordPerfect ignores all text strings that contain numbers and does not display them as errors.

6. When you see the message "Spell Check Completed," choose OK or press ↵.

To Check for Other Errors

1. From the Tools menu, choose Writing Tools (Alt-F1).
2. Choose Speller (1).
3. Choose Setup (Shift-F1).
4. Check one or more of these options: Check for Numbers in Words (3), Check for Double Words (4), or Check for Irregular Capitalization (5). Then select Close.
5. Continue from step 4 in the previous steps.

To Omit a Section from Spell-Checking

1. Select (block) the part of the document you do not want to spell-check.
2. From the Tools menu, choose Writing Tools (Alt-F1).
3. Choose Disable Speller/Grammatik (5).

Follow the steps to spell-check the document.

To Create or Edit a Supplemental Dictionary

You can create a supplemental dictionary to hold words and phrases you sometimes include in your documents but that WordPerfect would ordinarily not have in its main dictionary. For example, the names, company names, and addresses repeatedly included in your letters are good candidates for a supplemental dictionary.

1. From the Tools menu, choose Writing Tools (Alt-F1).
2. Choose Speller (1).
3. Choose Edit Supplemental Dictionary (6).
4. To create a new dictionary, choose Create New Sup, enter the file name for the dictionary, and press ↵. To Edit an

existing dictionary, highlight it in the list box and
choose Edit.

5. To add a new word, choose **A**dd (2) and select a word type
from the dialog box.

Word/Phrase to **S**kip (1)	Type the word or text string to skip and press ↵.
Word/Phrase with **R**eplacement (2)	Type a word or text string that you always want to replace in the **W**ord (1) text box and press ↵.. Then type a word or text string that should always be used as a replacement in the **R**eplacement (2) list box and press ↵. Then select OK to add the word and replacement to the list.
Word/Phrase with **A**lternates (3)	Type a word or text string that you always want WordPerfect to display and press ↵. Then, in the Add Alternate text box, type a word or text string that should be listed as a possible replacement and press ↵. Enter additional Alternates in the Add Alternate text box and press ↵ after each.

6. To edit a word, highlight the word in the list box and
choose **E**dit (1). Then make any changes in the text box(es)
and press ↵ or choose OK.

7. When you are finished, choose Close twice.

● **NOTES** The main WordPerfect dictionary is made up of word
lists; additional dictionaries in other languages can be purchased
from WordPerfect. You may also want to create or obtain a dictionary
that contains specialized terms for your industry.

You can use up to six main and six supplemental dictionaries at one
time by chaining them. Main dictionaries are provided by Word-
Perfect and other companies. Supplemental dictionaries are those
you or another WordPerfect user creates. Commands to chain dictionaries are in the Speller Setup dialog box.

● **SEE ALSO**   Language

SPREADSHEET

You can import data from a spreadsheet to a WordPerfect document in two ways. By importing part or all of the spreadsheet, the data is copied to the document. By linking to the spreadsheet, the data is copied and then can be updated in the document when changed in the spreadsheet.

To Import a Spreadsheet

1. Position the cursor where you want to enter the spreadsheet data.

2. From the Tools menu, choose Spreadsheet, and choose Import (Alt-F7,5,1).

3. Enter the name of the spreadsheet file in the Filename (1) text box and press ↵.

4. Choose Range (2), select the range of cells, and press ↵ to select only part of the spreadsheet.

5. Select the Type (3). You can import the spreadsheet as a Table or Text (2).

6. Choose Import.

When a spreadsheet is imported as a table, WordPerfect formats the table as close as it can to the original spreadsheet. When a spreadsheet is imported as text, WordPerfect formats the cells as columns separated by tabs, and the rows are separated by hard returns.

To Link to Spreadsheet Data

1. Position the cursor where you want to enter the spreadsheet data.

2. From the Tools menu, choose Spreadsheet, and choose Create Link (Alt-F7,5,2).

3. Enter the name of the spreadsheet file in the Filename (1) text box.

4. Choose Range (2), select the range of cells, and press ↵ to select only part of the spreadsheet.

5. Select the Type. You can import the spreadsheet as a Table (1) or Text (2).

6. Choose Link & Import to include the data and also link to the spreadsheet.

To Update Linked Data

1. From the Tools menu, choose Spreadsheet, and choose Link Options (Alt-F7,5,4).

2. To automatically update the spreadsheet data each time you open or retrieve the document, check Update on Retrieve (1) and choose OK. You can also leave Update on Retrieve not checked, and instead update the spreadsheet data manually by choosing Update All Links.

You can display (or hide) the link codes in your document in this Spreadsheet Link Options dialog box. To do so, use the Show Spreadsheet Link Codes (2) check box option. Link codes are displayed as comments.

● **NOTES**   You can delete a link without deleting the spreadsheet data by displaying the Reveal Codes window and deleting the code. You can delete the data by blocking it and pressing Delete.

You can import spreadsheets created with most versions of Plan-Perfect, Lotus 1-2-3, Microsoft Excel, Quattro, and Quattro Pro.

● **SEE ALSO**   Columns, Comments, Tabs, Tables

STYLES

Styles contain formatting information that can be applied repeatedly to paragraphs or blocks of text. Styles can be attached to and stored with a single document, or saved in a library and applied to other documents.

To Create a Style

1. From the Layout menu, choose Styles (Alt-F8).

2. Choose Create (2).

3. Enter a Style Name (1) in the text box and press ↵.

4. Select a Style Type (2) from the pop-up list:

Paragraph Style	The style is applied to the entire paragraph.
Character Style	The style is applied only to the selected (blocked) text or text beginning at the cursor location.
Open Style	The style is applied to the rest of the document beginning at the cursor location.

5. Check Create from Current Paragraph (3) if you want to use the formatting codes already in the paragraph. Or, check Create from Current Character if you want to use the font attributes already applied to the current or selected characters.

6. Choose OK or press ↵.

7. Choose Description (2), enter a description in the text box, and press ↵.

8. Choose Style Contents (4). Then define the style by pressing any of the keys shown or by choosing commands from the menus. When you are finished, press F7.

9. Select additional options, if necessary:

Show Style Off Codes (5)	A code and comment will appear in your document when the style ends.
Enter Key Action (6)	Choose an action from the list to specify the action when you select OK.

10. Choose OK.

11. If you want to select the style and apply it to the current selection, choose **S**elect (1). Or, choose Close.

To Apply a Style

1. Position the cursor anywhere in the paragraph (before selecting a paragraph style) or select the text (before selecting a character style).

2. From the Layout menu, choose **S**tyles (Alt-F8).

3. Highlight a Style Name in the list box and choose **S**elect (1).

If you make any formatting changes after you apply a style, those formatting changes override the style.

To End a Style

To turn off a paragraph style:

1. Position the cursor at the end of the paragraph.

2. From the Layout menu, choose **S**tyles (Alt-F8).

3. Highlight None in the list box and choose **S**elect (1).

To turn off a character style:

1. Position the cursor within the text.

2. From the Layout menu, choose **S**tyles (Alt-F8).

3. Choose **O**ff (1).

You can also delete a style from a section of text by displaying the Reveal Codes window and deleting the code.

To Modify a Style

1. From the Layout menu, choose Styles (Alt-F8).
2. Highlight a Style Name in the list box and choose Edit (3).
3. Choose Style Contents (4). Then modify the style by pressing any of the keys shown or by choosing commands from the menus. To delete a code, highlight it and press Delete. When you are finished, press F7.
4. Choose OK.
5. If you want to select the style and apply it to the current selection, highlight it and choose Select (1). Or, choose Close.

To Save Styles in a Library

1. From the Layout menu, choose Styles (Alt-F8).
2. Choose Save (7).
3. Enter a name in the Filename (1) text box. You may want to include a distinctive file extension, such as .STY, so you can recognize your style files.
4. Check the types of files you want to save.
5. Choose OK and then choose Close.

Style library files are saved in the directory you specify in Setup, Location of Files.

To Use Styles in a Library

To use styles in a library, retrieve that library. When you retrieve the library, all the styles in it are saved with the document.

1. From the Layout menu, choose Styles (Alt-F8).
2. Choose Retrieve (8).
3. Enter the library file name in the text box.
4. Check the types of files you want to retrieve.

5.   Choose OK.

● **NOTES**   A personal library contains the group of libraries you've created for your own use. A shared library is similar to this, but is stored in a common network directory that other users can access. Specify library locations with Setup, Location of Files. When naming library files, it's best to give each library a unique name that isn't duplicated at another location on the network.

When you open a new document, WordPerfect's default style library, which contains outline files, is always available. Word-Perfect also includes a sample library called LIBRARY.STY. These styles can be edited after they are copied by using the Copy command in the Style List dialog box.

Make sure Auto Code Placement is on when using styles.

● **SEE ALSO**   Auto Code Placement, Outline, Setup

TABLE OF AUTHORITIES

WordPerfect can generate a Table of Authorities from citations you mark, and it can be divided into sections based on citation type. A Table of Authorities is usually used in legal documents. For example, legal briefs cite specific cases and statutes. The Table of Authorities is a list that shows the page(s) on which these citations can be found.

To Mark a Full Form Citation

The first occurrence of a reference within a document is marked as a full form citation.

1.   Select (block) the text you want to cite.

2.   From the Tools menu, choose Table of Authorities, and then choose Mark Full (Alt-F5,3).

3. Choose Section Name (1), enter a number or name (for example, "Cases"), and press ↵. If you've previously defined the section names, choose List Sections (F5) and select from the list.

4. Choose Short Form (2), edit the text to the exact short form you want to use, and press ↵.

5. Choose Edit Full Form (3), edit the text so it is exactly as you want it to appear, and press F7.

6. Choose OK or press ↵.

Repeat the steps to mark each Table of Authorities full form citation. Once you've marked the full form, you can cite the references using the short form.

To Mark a Short Form Citation

Each subsequent occurrence of a reference within a document after a full form citation is marked as a short form citation.

1. Select (block) the text you want to cite.

2. From the Tools menu, choose Table of Authorities, and then choose Mark Short.

3. Edit the text in the Short Form text box so it is exactly as you want it to appear. Or choose List Short Forms (F5) and select from the list.

4. Choose OK or press ↵.

Repeat the steps to mark each Table of Authorities short form citation. When you are finished, define the Table of Authorities.

To Define the Table of Authorities

You can define the location for the Table of Authorities, the numbering format, and the sections you want it divided into.

1. Position the cursor at the location where you want the Table of Authorities to appear.

2. To begin the Table of Authorities on a new page, enter a page break by pressing Ctrl-↵.

3. Type the heading for the first section (for example, "Cases") and press ↵ to begin a new line.

4. From the Tools menu, choose Table of Authorities, and then choose Define (Alt-F5,2,3).

5. Highlight the section name you're defining and choose Edit (3).

6. Select an option from the Numbering Mode option box:

None (3)	No page numbers are included with the entries.
# Follows Entry (4)	The page numbers are placed after the entries.
(#) Follows Entry (5)	The page numbers are placed in parentheses after the entries.
# Flush Right (6)	The page numbers are right-justified.
...# Flush Right (7)	The page numbers are right-justified and preceded by dot leaders.

7. If you want to add an explanation to the page numbering format, choose Page Number Format (8) and select Different from Document (2). Choose Number Codes (F5), select a code from the dialog box, and choose OK.

8. Check Combine Sequential Page Numbers (9) if you want sequential page numbers combined instead of separated by commas.

9. Check Underlining Allowed (U) if you want WordPerfect to leave in any underlining in the marked text.

10. Choose OK or press ↵.

11. Choose Select (1).

Repeat the steps to define each additional section.

You should also renumber the pages beginning at the first page after the Table of Authorities. See the "Page Numbering" entry for those steps.

To Generate the Table of Authorities

After you've marked all the entries and also defined the Table of Authorities, follow the steps to generate it.

1. From the Tools menu, choose Generate (Alt-F5,4).

2. Choose OK or press ↵.

Remember to use Generate again after editing your document or Table of Authorities.

To Edit a Table of Authorities

1. From the Tools menu, choose Table of Authorities, and then choose Edit Full.

2. In the list box, highlight the short form for the citation you want to edit, and then do one or more of the following:

- Choose Short Form (1). Edit the text in the Short Form text box so it is exactly as you want it to appear and press ↵.
- Choose Full Form (3). Edit the text in the window so it is exactly as you want it to appear and press F7.
- Choose Section (2) to open the Define Table of Authorities dialog box and make changes to the Table of Authorities definition. Choose Close when you are finished.

3. Choose Close to close the dialog box.

● **NOTES**   To delete a Table of Authorities entry, display the Reveal Codes window and delete the ToA code. To delete a definition for a section, delete the Definition code. If you are working with a master document and subdocuments, define the Table of Authorities in the master document. You can create and modify Table of Authorities styles by choosing Styles (2) in the Edit Table of Authorities dialog box. From the Tools menu, choose Table of Authorities, choose Define, and choose Edit (Alt-F5,2,3,3). See the "Styles" entry for more information.

● **SEE ALSO** Master Document, Page Numbering, Reveal Codes, Styles

TABLE OF CONTENTS

WordPerfect can automatically generate a table of contents. A table of contents can include up to five levels of headings and subheadings.

To Mark Entries

1. Select (block) the text you want to insert as an entry.

2. From the Tools menu, choose Table of Contents and then choose **Mark** (Alt-F5,1).

3. Enter a level for the heading and choose OK or press ↵.

Repeat the steps to mark each Table of Contents entry. When you are finished, define the Table of Contents.

To Define the Table of Contents

You can define the location for the Table of Contents and the numbering format.

1. Position the cursor at the beginning of the document or at an alternate location where you want the Table of Contents to appear.

2. To begin the Table of Contents on a new page at the beginning of the document, enter a page break by pressing Ctrl-↵. Then press ↑ to move the cursor up to that new page.

3. Type **Table of Contents** and press ↵ to start a new line.

4. From the Tools menu, choose Table of Contents and then choose **Define** (Alt-F5,2,1).

5. Choose **N**umber of Levels (1), enter the number of levels you've used for marking Table of Contents entries, and press ↵.

6. Choose **L**evel (3), highlight the first style in the list, and then select a Numbering Mode from the options:

None (1)	No page numbers are included with the entries.
# Follows Entry (2)	The page numbers are placed after the entries.
(#) Follows Entry (3)	The page numbers are placed in parentheses after the entries.
# Flush Right (4)	The page numbers are right-justified.
...# Flush Right (5)	The page numbers are right-justified and preceded by dot leaders.

7. Check **W**rap the Last Level (4) if you want the last heading level wrapped flush left, instead of indented (the default) in a multilevel Table of Contents.

8. Choose **P**age Number format (5) to change the page numbering format, and select **D**ifferent from Document (2). Choose Number Codes (F5), select a code from the dialog box, and choose OK. Press ↵ when the correct codes are in the Different from Document dialog box.

9. Choose OK or press ↵ until all dialog boxes are closed.

You may also want to renumber the pages beginning at the first page after the Table of Contents. See the "Page Numbering" entry for those steps.

To Generate the Table of Contents

After you've marked all the entries and also defined the Table of Contents, follow these steps to generate it:

1. From the **T**ools menu, choose **G**enerate (Alt-F5,4).

2. Choose OK or press ↵.

Remember to use Generate again after editing your document and before printing it.

● **NOTES**   To delete a Table of Contents entry, display the Reveal Codes window and delete the Mark Text code. To delete the Table of Contents definition, delete the Definition code.

If you are working with a master document and subdocuments, define the Table of Contents in the master document.

When you check Wrap the Last Level (4), the consecutive last level headings appear on the same line instead of being separated by a line break. Flush Right and Flush Left numbering are not available for these entries.

You can create and modify Table of Contents styles by choosing Table of Contents Styles (2) in the Define Table of Contents dialog box. See the "Styles" entry for more information.

● **SEE ALSO**   Master Document, Page Numbering, Reveal Codes, Styles

TABLES

A table is a group of rows and columns into which you can enter text, numbers, formulas, and functions.

To Create a Table

1.   From the Layout menu, choose Tables, and choose Create (Alt-F7,2,1).

2.   Enter the number of columns and rows you want in the table and choose OK. (See "To Edit a Table" if you want to edit the table now.)

3.   Choose Close (F7). The Table Edit dialog box must be closed before you can type within the table.

Table 14: Moving Around a Table

Keys	Moves the Cursor
↓	To the next row.
↑	To the previous row.
→	One column to the right if the column contains no text; or one character to the right.
←	One column to the left if the column contains no text; or one character to the left.
Tab	One column to the right.
Shift-Tab	One column to the left.
Ctrl-Home	To any cell location you enter.
Home, Home ↑	To the first cell.
Home, Home ↓	To the last cell.

4.   Enter the text and data in each cell, but do not press ↵ at the end of each entry. Use the keys in Table 14 to move around the table or, with the mouse, click in any cell to move there.

To Convert Text to a Table

If you have text formatted as tabular or parallel columns, you can convert it to a table.

1.   Select (block) the text you want to convert.

2.   From the Layout menu, choose Tables, and then choose Create (Alt-F7,2,1).

3.   Select the type of text, either Tabular Text (1) or Parallel Columns (2), and choose OK.

4.   Choose Close (F7). The Table Edit dialog box must be closed before you can type within the table.

To Modify a Table

1.   Position the cursor anywhere within the table.

2.   From the Layout menu, choose Tables, and choose Edit (Alt-F11).

3.   Follow any of these steps to modify the table's format:

- Press Ctrl-→ to increase the width of the current column.

- Press Ctrl-← to decrease the width of the current column.

- Press Insert or choose Ins to insert a row or column, and then make selections in the dialog box and choose OK.

- Press Delete or choose Del to delete the current row or column, and then make selections in the dialog box and choose OK.

- Choose Move/Copy to move or copy the current row, column, or cell, and then make selections in the dialog box.

- Choose Cell (1), Column (2), Row (3), or Table (4) to modify its format, make selections in the dialog box, and choose OK. Choose Number Type (6) in the Cell, Column, or Table Format dialog box to change the format for numbers in part or all of the table.

- Choose Lines/Fill (6) to add lines, borders, and fills to part or all of the table, and then make selections in the dialog box and choose Close. See the "Borders" and "Graphics Lines" entries for more information.

4.   When you have finished modifying the format, choose Close (F7) in the Table Edit dialog box.

To Enter a Formula or Function

1.   Position the cursor in the first cell where you want to enter a formula or calculation.

2. From the Layout menu, choose Tables, and then choose Edit (Alt-F11).

3. Choose Formula (5).

4. Enter the Formula (1) in the text box and press ↵. Formulas can include the common mathematical symbols (+, –, ∗, and ?/) as well as those listed in Table 15. Or, choose Functions (F5), highlight a function in the list box, and choose Insert.

5. Include any arguments in the Formula list box. The dialog box displays an example of the arguments that should be entered with each function.

6. Check Formula Recognition at Document Level (2).

7. Choose OK.

8. To calculate the formula, choose Calc.

Table 15: Formulas for Calculating in Tables

Formula Character	Result
+ (subtotal)	The numbers in the cells above it are added
= (total)	The subtotals in the cells above it are added
∗ (grand total)	The totals in the cells above it are added

To Delete a Table

- To delete entries within cells, block the cells and press Delete.

- To delete a table, select (block) the entire table and press Delete.

To Insert a Tab

Since the Tab key is used to move around a table, you'll need to use these keys to insert a tab within a cell.

- To insert a right tab, press Home-Alt-F6.

- To insert a left tab, press Home-Tab.

- To insert a decimal tab, press Home-Ctrl-F6.

- To insert a center tab, press Home-Shift-F6.

● **NOTES**   Use Block Protect to prevent a table that is less than one-page long from being split. To insert a page break in a table, position the cursor inside the table and press Ctrl-⏎. The page break is inserted before the current row. If you create a table that is wider than the width of the paper you have selected, WordPerfect prints only the information that fits on the page. You can use styles to format a table.

● **SEE ALSO**   Block, Borders, Columns, Font Attributes, Graphics Lines, Math, Styles

TABS

Use Tabs to move a single line or the first line of a paragraph a specific amount or to set up simple columns.

To Insert Tabs and Back Tabs

- Press Tab to begin the line at the next tab stop.

- Press Shift-Tab to begin the line at the previous tab stop.

To Change the Tab Settings

1. Position the cursor where you want to begin the tab setting change.

2. From the Layout menu, choose Tab Set.

3. To delete a tab setting, press → to move the cursor to a tab and choose Clear One or press Delete. Or, to delete all the tab settings, choose Clear All or press Ctrl-End.

4. To set a new tab, first select Absolute or Relative. Absolute tabs are measured from the left edge of the page and never change. Relative tabs are measured from the left margin and change when the margin is changed.

5. Select either Left, Right, Center, or Decimal, based on the type of tab you're creating.

6. Type the location for the tab in the Set Tab text box and press ↵. Or, double-click the location for the tab in the ruler. You can also set evenly spaced tabs by selecting Repeat Every, entering the distance in the text box, and pressing ↵.

7. Select Dot Leader to place a dot leader between the tabs.

8. Choose OK.

• **NOTES**   Use Indents to move an entire paragraph in from the margin. Use Columns or Tables to format large blocks of text in multiple columns instead of separating text with tabs. Display the Reveal Codes window if you want to see the tab settings in the document window.

See the "Decimal Alignment" entry to change the Decimal Alignment character. Change the Dot Leader Character by choosing Character from the Layout menu and entering a new character in the Dot Leader Character text box.

• **SEE ALSO**   Columns, Decimal Alignment, Indent, Reveal Codes, Tables

TEXT MODE

When you work in Text mode, WordPerfect displays the body of your document text in a nonproportional typeface, no matter what font or point size you have selected for the text. Font attributes are displayed in the color you have specified with the Setup Display command. Graphics are not displayed; WordPerfect shows only their location on the screen.

To Work in Text Mode

Text mode is starred on the menu when active. To select it, from the View menu choose Text Mode (Ctrl-F3,2). Figure 17 shows the main elements of the document window available for display when Text mode is active.

● **NOTES**   When entering text into a complex document that contains many font and formatting changes, tables and/or graphics, switch to Text mode if you are experiencing delays. In Text mode,

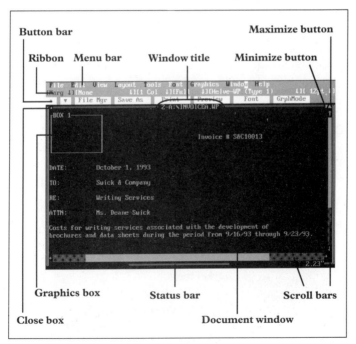

Figure 17: The Text mode window

headers, footers, footnotes and endnotes are not displayed. Use Page mode or select Print Preview if you want to see them.

- **SEE ALSO**   Graphics Mode, Page Mode, Print Preview

THESAURUS

Use the Thesaurus to look up and replace words with their synonyms or antonyms.

To Use the Thesaurus

1. Position the cursor anywhere in the word that you want to look up.

2. From the Tools menu, choose Writing Tools (Alt-F1).

3. Choose Thesaurus (2).

4. Highlight a replacement word in the list box and choose Replace.

Thesaurus Options

These options are available with the Thesaurus:

Look Up	Lets you list synonyms and antonyms for a word in the list box or any word you enter in the Word text box.
View	Displays your document in the top half of the screen and the Thesaurus in the bottom. Press F7 to return to the Thesaurus.
Clear Column	Clears the current list box and moves each column to the left. Use Clear Column as often as needed to clear the screen.

| History | Displays a list box with the words you have looked up since you opened the Thesaurus dialog box. |

● **NOTES**   Word listings are organized into *headwords*, *references*, and *subgroups*. The headword is the word at the top of the column that has been looked up. References are words listed below and labeled as nouns (n), verbs (v), adjectives (a), or antonyms (ant). Words marked with a bullet (●) can be looked up. Beneath the references are one or more subgroups, which are words with the same general meaning.

TYPEOVER MODE

When WordPerfect is in Typeover mode, the characters and spaces you insert replace, or "type over," existing characters and spaces.

To Select Typeover Mode

WordPerfect is normally in Insert mode. To switch to Typeover mode, press Insert. When WordPerfect is in Typeover mode, the word *Typeover* is displayed in the status bar at the left. Characters you type replace characters and spaces, but codes are not replaced (with the exception of Tab codes). Table 16 shows the keys that are affected when you switch to Typeover mode.

● **NOTES**   If you unintentionally delete text while in Typeover mode, you can choose Undo (Ctrl-Z) or Undelete (Esc) from the Edit menu to restore it. Typeover mode is always active when you are using Line Draw.

● **SEE ALSO**   Insert Mode, Line Draw, Undelete, Undo

Table 16: Key Changes in Typeover Mode

Key	Action
Backspace	The character to the left of the cursor is replaced by a space.
Spacebar	The character at the cursor is replaced by a space.
Tab	The cursor is positioned at the next tab stop on the line. If none exists, a tab is inserted.
Shift-Tab	The cursor is positioned at the previous tab stop on the line. If the cursor is at the left margin, a back tab is inserted.

UNDELETE

Undelete lets you restore the last three text or graphic items you've deleted.

To Recover Deleted Text or Graphics

1. Position the cursor where you want to restore the text or on the page where you want to restore the graphic.

2. From the Edit menu, choose Undelete (Esc).

3. To restore the last deleted item, choose **R**estore (1). To restore a previous deletion, choose **P**revious Deletion (2) once or twice until WordPerfect displays the text or graphic you want to restore, and then choose **R**estore (1).

● **NOTES**   Undelete always restores the text at the current cursor location and a graphics box at its previous location on the current page. To restore an item to its original location, use Undo.

· ● **SEE ALSO**   Undo

UNDERLINE

You can underline or double-underline selected text or new text.

To Underline Text

1.   If you haven't yet typed the text, position the cursor where you want to begin underlining. If you've already entered the text, select (block) the text you want to underline.

2.   From the Font menu, choose Underline (F8) or Double Underline.

To start typing normal text after you finish typing the text you wanted underlined, choose Normal (Ctrl-N) from the Font menu.

● **NOTES**   If you are applying other attribute changes to the text, as well as underlining, it is quickest to make all the changes in the Font dialog box. In Text mode, underlining appears as highlighted text, provided you have not changed the settings with Setup, Display.

● **SEE ALSO**   Font Attributes, Setup

You can reverse many editing actions with Undo. For example, you can restore text to its original location, restore deleted font attributes, delete newly applied attributes, and reset margins and tabs.

To Undo an Operation

To cancel the effects of the previous editing action, from the Edit menu choose Undo (Ctrl-Z).

To Turn on Undo

If Undo is dimmed on the menu, you need to turn it on.

1. From the File menu choose Setup, and then choose Environment (Shift-F1,3).

2. Check Allow Undo (4).

3. Choose OK or press ↵. If you pressed (Shift-F1,3), select Close or press ↵ again.

Some operations take more time when Undo is allowed.

● **NOTES** Undo always restores text and graphics to their original location. Use Undelete to restore them to another location. You cannot undo cursor movements or most complex operations, including sort or merge text. However, you can undo a select operation.

● **SEE ALSO**   Setup, Sort and Select, Undelete

UNITS OF MEASURE

You can change the way WordPerfect displays and you enter numbers from inches, which is the default, to centimeters, millimeters, points, 1200ths of an inch, or WP 4.2 units.

To Change the Default Units of Measure

1. From the File menu choose Setup, and then choose Environment (Shift-F1,3).

2. Choose Units of Measure (7).

3. Choose Display/Entry of Numbers (1) and select a setting from the pop-up box.

4. Choose Status Line Display (2) and select a setting from the pop-up box.

5. Choose OK or press ↵ twice. If you used (Shift-F1,3), you must also select Close or press ↵ a third time.

● **SEE ALSO** Setup

N E W
WATERMARKS

You can add multiple watermarks to a document, using either graphics or text. A *watermark* is placed behind the body of the document on each page and printed in a lighter shade (gray on non-color printers).

To Create a Watermark

1.   Position the cursor anywhere on the page where you want to insert a watermark.

2.   From the Layout menu, choose Header/Footer/Watermark.

3.   Select Watermarks (3), and select the first watermark, **A** or **B** (1 or 2), that you want to create.

4.   Select whether to show the watermark on **A**ll (1), **E**ven (2), or **O**dd (3) pages, and then choose **C**reate.

5.   Either type the watermark or enter a graphic.

- Type the text of the watermark. Use the commands on the Font menu to modify the appearance of the text. WordPerfect's editing keys and commands are available in this window. Press F7 to close the editing window when you are finished.

- From the **G**raphics menu, choose Graphics **B**oxes, and then choose **C**reate (Alt-F9,1,1). Choose **F**ilename (1), enter a file name in the text box, and press ⏎. Then choose Image Editor (3) and edit the image. Press F7 to close the Image Editor when you are finished.

6.   If you're creating a graphic watermark, choose OK or press ⏎ to close the Create Graphics Box dialog box. Then press F7 to close the editing window.

You can see the watermarks on your screen only by choosing Print Preview (Shift-F7,7).

To Edit a Watermark

1.   From the Layout menu, choose Header/Footer/Watermark.

2.   To turn off the watermark, select Watermarks **A** or **B** (3, 1 or 2), and choose Off.

3.   To edit the contents, select the watermark you want to edit and choose Edit.

4.   Edit the watermark if it is a text watermark. Press F7 to close the editing window when you are finished. Or, from

the **G**raphics menu, choose Graphics **B**oxes and choose
Edit (Alt-F9,1,2). Choose **E**dit Box and make changes in
this dialog box. Choose Image **E**ditor (3) to edit the image.
Press F7 to close the Image Editor when you are finished.

5. If you're editing a graphic watermark, choose OK or press
↵ to close the Edit Graphics Box dialog box. Then press F7
to close the editing window.

To Delete a Watermark

To delete a watermark, position the cursor at the beginning of the
document, display the Reveal Codes window, and delete the code.
If you have multiple watermarks, you can first position the cursor
on the code to read its contents before deleting the code.

● **NOTES**   You can include up to two watermarks on any page
in your document. WordPerfect labels them Watermark A and B in
order to keep track of them, but the letters have no significance. You
can change a watermark within your document by turning it off and
creating a new one. Suppress a watermark on one or more pages by
using the Page command on the Layout menu (Shift-F8).

● **SEE ALSO**   Font Attributes, Image Editor, Page Format,
Reveal Codes

WIDOWS AND ORPHANS

You can prevent WordPerfect from inserting a page break that
causes the last line of a paragraph to be placed at the top of a page
(called a *widow*) or the first line of a paragraph to be placed at the
bottom of a page (called an *orphan*).

To Prevent Widows and Orphans

1. From the **L**ayout menu, choose **O**ther (Shift-F8,7).

WP DOS

2.   Check Widow/Orphan Protect (3).

3.   Choose OK or press ⏎. If you used (Shift-F8,7), press ⏎ again or select Close.

● **NOTES**   The Block Protect feature lets you mark a block of text and keep it on the same page. The Conditional End of Page feature lets you keep a specific number of lines together on a page.

● **SEE ALSO**   Block, Conditional End of Page

WINDOWS

You can have up to nine document windows open at one time, and you can display as many of them as you need while keeping others temporarily hidden in the background.

The maximum size of the document window depends on the other elements you have displayed on the screen. If you are displaying the menu bar, ribbon, button bar and/or scroll bars, the document window area is smaller than it would be if none of these items were displayed. Figure 18 shows four document windows tiled on the screen, with only the status bar on the bottom. The current window is the one that contains the cursor.

To Switch to another Window

A document window is opened when you start WordPerfect. Additional windows are opened when you use the Open or New command. When more than one window is open, use these techniques to make another window the current or active window.

● Click in any part of a window to make it the active window.

● From the Window menu, choose Next (Ctrl-F3,1,6) to make the next window in sequence active.

● From the Window menu, choose Previous (Ctrl-F3,1,7) to make the previous window in sequence active.

Close box Title bar Minimize button Maximize button

Active window

Figure 18: Tiled Windows

- From the Window menu, choose Switch (Shift-F3) to make the last window you used active, or choose Switch repeatedly to toggle two windows.

- From the Window menu, choose Switch to (F3) to see a list of open windows, and select a number from the list.

To Frame a Window

From the Window menu, choose Frame (Ctrl-F3,1,2) to place a border around a maximized window. When windows are minimized, tiled, or cascaded, frames are automatically placed around them. Once a window is framed, you can drag its borders to resize it or drag its title bar to move it.

To Arrange Windows

- Place the mouse pointer on the title bar of any framed window and drag the window to another location.

- From the **W**indow menu, choose **T**ile (Ctrl-F3,1,4) to arrange windows so that you can see all open windows on the screen.

- From the **W**indow menu, choose **C**ascade (Ctrl-F3,1,5) to arrange windows so that you can see only the active open window and the title bars of the remaining open windows.

- Choose **M**ove (Ctrl-F3,1,9), press ↑, ↓, →, or ← to move the active window in any direction, and press ↵.

To Size Windows

- Place the mouse pointer on the sides or bottom edge of any framed window and drag the edges in or out to make the window smaller or larger.

- Place the mouse pointer on any corner and drag the corner in or out to make the window proportionally smaller or larger.

- Choose **S**ize (Ctrl-F3,1,S), press ↑, ↓, →, or ← to make the current window smaller or larger, and press ↵.

- To reduce the size of the current window to a small rectangle, from the **W**indow menu choose Minimize (Ctrl-F3,1,1), or simply click the window's Minimize button.

- To increase the size of the current window to the full width of the document window, from the **W**indow menu choose **M**aximize (Ctrl-F3,1,3), or simply click the window's Maximize button. When you maximize a window, the frame is removed and all other windows are hidden.

To Close a Window

- When displaying windows with frames, click the Close box of each window you want to close.

- From the File menu, choose Close.

If the document in the window has changed since you last saved it, you'll be prompted to save it. If it has not changed, it will be closed immediately.

● **NOTES**   You can use Screen Setup to establish your preferences for screen and window elements. Although WordPerfect lets you open as many as nine document windows, how many windows you can open is limited by the amount of memory in your computer.

● **SEE ALSO**   Button Bar, Exit Document/Exit WP/Close, Menus, Ribbon, Screen Setup, Scroll Bars

WORD COUNT

WordPerfect counts and calculates not only the number of words, but also the number of characters, sentences, and pages in a document.

To Count Words

1. To count words in part of a document, select (block) the section of the document. To count the words in an entire document, make it the current document by opening it or switching to the document window.

2. From the Tools menu, choose Writing Tools, and choose Document Information (Alt-F1,4).

3. WordPerfect calculates and displays the information in a dialog box.

4. To close the dialog box, choose OK or press ↵.

● **SEE ALSO** Block, Document Information, Open, Windows

WP CHARACTERS

The WP Characters command lets you insert many different symbols and foreign characters into your documents.

To Insert a Special Character

1. Position the cursor where you want to insert the character.

2. From the Font menu, choose WP Characters (Ctrl-W).

3. If you know the number of the character you want to insert, you can enter the number in the Number text box (1), press ↵, and skip the remaining steps. If you don't know the number and it isn't in the current set, press Esc, select Set (2), and select a character set from the pop-up box. There are a number of character sets to choose from.

4. Select Characters (3) and use the arrow keys or click with the mouse to highlight a character in the list box. You can select and insert the character by double-clicking on it.

5. If you are using keystrokes, choose Insert.

● **NOTES** You can apply most font attributes to special characters. You also can use Overstrike to combine and create special characters.

● **SEE ALSO** Font Attributes, Overstrike

Use Zoom to change the displayed size of text and graphics in the document window. Zoom affects the way a document is displayed but has no affect on how it is printed. Zoom is not available in Text mode.

To Change the Screen Magnification

1. From the View menu, choose Zoom.

2. Select from the available options to specify a degree of magnification for text and graphics in the document window.

50%, 75%	Text and graphics are reduced in size so you can view more of the page on your screen.
100%	Text and graphics are displayed close to the size at which they will print.
125%, 150%, 200%	Text and graphics are increased in size so you can view and edit them more easily.
Margin Width	The left and right margins of the document are displayed at the left and right edges of the document window.
Page Width	The left and right edges of the page are displayed at the left and right edges of the document window.

Full Page   The top and bottom edges of the
                             page are displayed at the top and
                             bottom edges of the document
                             window, so you can see a full page
                             of your document at one time.

You can also select a different setting from the Zoom drop-down list
box, which is available from the Ribbon.

● **NOTES**   Use Screen Setup to change the default setting for
Zoom.

● **SEE ALSO**   Ribbon, Screen Setup

Index

Note to the reader:
This index uses **boldface** to indicate primary discussions of a subject.

234   Index

236 Index

Help Yourself with Another Quality Sybex Book

Delete Keys

Keys	Description
Delete	Deletes the current character
Backspace	Deletes the character to the left
Ctrl-Backspace	Deletes the current word
Ctrl-End	Deletes the rest of the line
Ctrl-PgDn	Deletes the remainder of a page

Function Keys

Command	Keys
Block	Alt-F4 *or* F12
Bold	F6
Bookmark	Shift-F12
Cancel	Esc
Center	Shift-F6
Columns	Alt-F7
Date	Shift-F5
Decimal Tab	Ctrl-F6
End Field	F9
Envelope	Alt-F12
Exit	F7
Fax	Shift-F7
File Manager	F5
Flush Right	Alt-F6
Font	Ctrl-F8
Format	Shift-F8
Graphics	Alt-F9
Help	F1
Indent, Double	Shift-F4
Indent, Left	Shift-Tab